The World's First Non-Fiction Cookbook

by Ben Levitan

► Too Easy Gourmet Press
P.O. Box 469
Annapolis, MD 21404

Illustrations and graphic design by Ruth Bielobocky

Printed in the United States of America—First Edition.
Library of Congress Catalog Number: 94-90329

ISBN 0-9640023-0-2

10 9 8 7 6 5 4 3 2

▼

What others are saying about this book...

▶ "Ben can cook! And with this delightful book, so can you...with just five ingredients and a few minutes! This is my favorite kind of cooking: simple, healthful, and fast!"

Martin Yan
Television Host,"Yan Can Cook"

▶ "Ben Levitan has created a cookbook which cuts to the quick of recipe presentation, creating a cookbook for people on the run. Using the Levitan approach, every family can have a nutritious, tasty and interesting meal on the table on the most hectic days. As an example of Levitan's succinct style we will quote his recipe for "Apple Compote" which is a quick no-nonsense fruit dessert."

America On-Line
In "Finest Cookbooks On-line"

▶ "Ben's approach is fantastic.You can make gourmet meals in short order time at fast food prices."

Merle Ellis, the Butcher
Television Host, "Cookin' USA"

▶ "TOO EASY GOURMET is almost too good to be true—great recipes that are simple, fast, and that also taste good. This book is a winner!"

Bill Cates, Past President
The American Cooking Guild

▶ "No cookbook demonstrates more easily, realistic and understandable approaches to preparing healthy gourmet dishes."

Melvin Murphy
Author of *Desire:
The Emotional Appetite
For Success*

▶ "I have nothing but compliments for your recipes. The book is great, and incredibly easy to use. And you're right—the food turns out just as you said it would—terrific tasting and healthy—and with so few ingredients. Where was this book when I was a college student or better yet as a newlywed in a dual career family? You really have a great approach to cooking!"

Paul Knott
President, Center for
Effective Organizations

▶ "Wow—Simple and streamlined, easy and exotic (Vermouth hamburger!) This is a godsend for anyone who ever wanted to celebrate good taste without sacrificing all day."

Maggie Bedrosian
Author: *LIFE is More
Than Your To-Do List*

▶ "Ben adds a new dimension to 'fast food'—quick-to-prepare recipes you can do yourself. And the recipes are healthy, too."

Anne Marie Schissler
President, Lifestyle Wellness

▶ "On first seeing TOO EASY GOURMET my wife Lu thought she might put it under my pillow so I could learn to cook by osmosis. But, after I dipped into it, especially the Intro and the Shopping Strategies I've resolved to learn a few [recipes] and surprise everyone—especially myself —with my skillet skills."

John Jay Daly
Chevy Chase, MD

▶ "What a great resource! For the busy single or couple this book is a must. Few ingredients, quick preparation and the recipes have nutrition information with calories and fat content, exactly what people need today. What more could you want?"

Washington Jewish Week
Washington D.C.

▶ "I made your macaroni and cheese recipe for my son and we licked the bowl clean! It was great and I was so proud of myself because it was fresh, not frozen or from a box!"

Sue Cummings
Alexandria, VA

▶ "No more carry out for my family! We've fallen in love with TOO EASY GOURMET!"

Lynne Waymon
Author of How To
Fireproof Your Career

▶ "Ben's book is a welcome paradigm shift in cooking! It's about time."

Rae Thompson
Business Writer/Consultant

Table of Contents

Acknowledgements

This book would not have been possible without the support of so
many people including: editors, Gary Gordon, and Sandra Nortman;
indexer Larry Harrison; proofers, Ann Longknife and Lisa Katzman,
assistant, Kay McFadden; graphic designer and illustrator, Ruth Bielobocky.
Also, thanks to members of the National Speakers Association,
numerous tasters, and everyone who ever took my cooking
workshop and asked the question "Do you have a book!?"

▼

Foreword

The "Yan Can Cook Show" is now in its fifteenth year, reaching television audiences all over the world. During that decade-and-a-half, I've seen a lot of changes in the kinds of recipes people are looking for, and I've tried to respond to those changes in both my show and my cookbooks. What people seem to need and want today are simple recipes with fewer ingredients—recipes that are economical and quick to prepare, but still healthful and packed with flavor. In other words, they want it all...they're expecting a miracle!

That's where Ben Levitan comes in.

Ben is a master of the art of the simple, successful recipe. I've developed plenty of recipes for myself for one or two people over the years. But in this book, and in his cooking workshops, Ben starts with this premise. He understands the needs of the busy home cook who has just a few minutes to put dinner together. No matter who you are or how much cooking experience you have, with this book and a few basic ingredients, you can make meals that are good for you and good tasting any day of the week.

I've made it my mission to introduce home cooks to the fun and excitement of preparing simple foods. That's why I always end my show by saying "If Yan can cook, so can you," Well, Ben can cook, too. And, with a little inspiration from the book, so can you! Enjoy!

Martin Yan
Host, "Yan Can Cook"

Introduction

Most cookbooks are like the new Paris fashions. They're great to look at, but they're just too much trouble for everyday wear. At best you pull them out for the weekend or special occasions. Like fashion, men will learn one recipe and pull it out for every special occasion. Women like new recipes for every event, much like the socialite who fears being seen twice in the same dress.

Today the average family size is 2.6 people (70% singles, or couples, or single parents) cooking for one or two, so why do most cookbooks and classes still teach meals for 6-8 people that often take hours to prepare (Do these guys have jobs?) and cost $20 for 1 serving (called frugal and budget?) and leave you with a fridge full of left over ingredients? (despite being called Quick and Easy)!

Too Easy Gourmet has a new approach to cooking. Too Easy Gourmet offers quick, easy and healthy meals for every day after eight busy hours and an equally hard commute home. It's your first non-fiction cookbook!

Too Easy Gourmet recipes are all:

- 20 minutes or less to make (including prep time). There are no overnight marinades or four hour simmers.

- Recipes with 5 or fewer ingredients (full meals are often 10 items or less).

- Made from common, non-branded ingredients found at your grocery store.

- Healthy because the recipes show fat grams for every key ingredient and also explain what they mean to your overall diet.

- Budget conscious. No catches, like expensive equipment. All you need is a simple pan or two. (No dehydrators, Kitchen Wiz, or other "infomercial" wonder tool).

- Designed for one or two. Few, if any leftovers or extra ingredients that go to waste.

- Fun & creative. You'll impress your guests and yourself

These 100, very well-tested, good tasting, healthy and inexpensive recipes will make YOU the Too Easy Gourmet!

▼

How to Use This Book

The goal of this book is to help you develop a repertoire of easy meals you can make without thinking. You likely have secondary goals as well—such as losing weight, saving money, or learning to entertain guests.

The best approach is to start with the first recipe and try each one exactly as described. Make it a goal to try at least one recipe a week. Each recipe requires five ingredients or fewer and if you use the shopping strategies on page 106 you'll only spend a few dollars at the most. (If you randomly try recipes you will likely miss some delicious surprises.) This approach will have you trying things you normally wouldn't. You won't like every recipe in this book, but likewise you will find some new things that you'll love. In either case, it will cost you very little time and money to find out, so you'll stay motivated.

You soon will find a handful of recipes you like and find easy to prepare. After making those a few times you will be able to fix them on the spur of the moment without using the recipe.

If you are particularly interested in losing weight read page 112, Diet & Nutrition. Notice that the fat content of every recipe and every key ingredient is listed on the same page as the recipe.

If you are particularly interested in saving money, look at page 106, Shopping Strategies.

If you are having guests for dinner tonight, turn to page 2, and make the meal and suggested accompaniments. Also, page 115 has more suggested meals.

After you work through the main courses, start cooking full meals by adding side dishes, then appetizers, then desserts. If you find side dishes you particularly like, you can double them and have them as main courses. Page 115 also suggests some full meals.

The "serve with" information found on main course recipes contains suggestions for a full meal. The "serve with" information on side dishes, starters and desserts indicate several main courses these items would go well with.

Terminology. Notice that many recipes contain terms with quotes around them. These terms are defined on page 109.

All recipes are for one. If you are cooking for more than one, simply double/triple the recipe, keeping everything else the same. (See Measurements p.114.)

Substituting ingredients Always do the recipe exactly as described the first time you make it to understand how it is supposed to look and taste. After the first time, if you want to make changes to suit your tastes, definitely do! But make small changes each time until you have personalized the recipe. (Example: changing from butter to margarine, the first time, then adding a little of a new spice the next time, etc.) Don't forget to mark the changes in the recipe book so you'll remember.

Remember, the goal is to save you time and make your life easier.

Equipment: You'll only need a few things to make these recipes. First a frypan or skillet, which is a shallow pan preferably with a non-stick lining; and a sauce pan, which is a deep pot that could hold about 1 quart of liquid and a spatula or wooden spoon.

The best way to be successful with these recipes is to buy fresh ingredients, and have them measured and ready (laid out on the kitchen counter) before you start.

Maybe in the future, supermarkets will pack the four or five ingredients you need in nice neat plastic trays marked Too Easy Gourmet with the recipe attached, but until then you still have to shop!

Make sure you have read the recipe carefully, and then follow it. After you cook, make notes on the page to help yourself out next time. Mark recipes you particularly liked.

Make your life easier too by keeping the few pans, utensils, plates, silverware and measuring tools you need together, clean and ready to use.

Enjoy this book, and may it free your time, have you feeling healthy, and make cooking fun for you!

Main Courses

▼

Lemon Chicken

Ingredients:

One 1/4 lb. Chicken Breast (skinless, boneless)

2 teaspoons Butter

Juice from 1/2 Lemon

1 teaspoon Parsley, chopped

Instructions:

Place chicken between two sheets of wax paper & pound evenly to a 1/4" thickness. Melt butter in pan over medium heat until bubbly. Add the chicken and sauté two minutes per side. Remove the cooked chicken to a warm plate, and "deglaze" pan with lemon juice. Add parsley, stir quickly and pour over chicken as sauce. Serve.

Comments:

A single 4 oz. Chicken Breast (1/4 lb.) is about right for this recipe. Also, roll the Lemon on the counter top to get more juice out of it. Time for this meal: 6 minutes! Shopping Tip: Buy a single Chicken Breast already skinned and boned for fast and cost-effective preparation. (Are you really going to de-bone a whole chicken and save the bones for chicken stock?) See page 106 for more tips.

Nutritional Information:

	Chicken	Butter	Lemon
Fat 11.31 g	3.1	8.2	.01
Calories	142	74	9
Fat Percent	20%	100%	1%

Serve with:

Sesame Broccoli (p. 34)

Parsley Pasta (p. 40)

Le Colonel (p. 87)

Pasta Quick

Ingredients:

1 14.5 oz can Whole Tomatoes, drained & chopped

1 clove Garlic, minced

2 teaspoons brown Sugar

1/2 teaspoon Oregano

3 cups cooked Pasta

Instructions:

Chop first four ingredients and stir over medium heat for about 5 minutes. (Do not allow to boil.) You can add 1 teaspoon butter for extra flavor. Serve over the cooked pasta.

Comments:

The consistency of the sauce can be varied from fine to chunky. Blend well for a fine sauce and a short time for a chunky sauce.

Nutritional Information:

	Tomato	Sugar	Butter
Fat 4.1 g	0	0	4.1
Calories	25	30	37
Fat Percent	0%	0%	100%

Serve with

Sesame Broccoli (p. 34)
Mandarin Spinach Salad (p. 62)
Le Colonel (p. 87)

Veal Piccata

Ingredients:

2 Veal cutlets Scaloppini (about 4 oz.)

2 tablespoons Flour

1 teaspoon Olive Oil

1 small clove Garlic, crushed

2 tablespoons Lemon Juice (about 1/2 Lemon)

Instructions:

Heat olive oil in small saucepan over medium heat. Dredge veal in flour and place immediately in pan. Cook 2 minutes per side, 4 minutes total. Remove to plate. Remove pan from heat. Add garlic and lemon juice. "Deglaze" pan slowly and pour sauce over veal.

Comments:

1 tablespoon white wine added to the sauce during deglazing is also a nice touch. And, if you prefer, you can heat sauce slightly to reduce it to a medium texture.

Nutritional Information:

	Veal	Flour	Oil
Fat 17.24 g	12.5	.14	4.6
Calories	246	52.5	41.6
Fat Percent	46%	2%	100%

Serve with:

Parsley Pasta (p. 40)

Mandarin Spinach Salad (p. 62)

Amaretto Strawberries (p. 86)

Foiled Again Fillets

Ingredients:

1/2 lb. Haddock Fillets

1 tablespoon Butter

1/2 cup Onion (small Onion)

Juice from 1/2 Lemon

Instructions:

Preheat oven to 400°. Place the fish, skin side down, on a piece of aluminum foil large enough to fully wrap the fish. Top with the chopped onions, butter (cut in small pieces over the fish) and lemon juice. Wrap the package and place in the oven for 19 minutes. When finished, open package and gently transfer to serving plate.

Comments:

A half pound haddock fillet (about a 9" piece of fillet) is boneless and usually still has the skin on one side. This will flake off after cooking.

Nutritional Information:

	Haddock	Butter	Onion	Lemon
Fat 13.8 g	1.2	12.3	.2	.1
Calories	158	111	27	8
Fat Percent	7%	100%	7%	11%

Serve with:

Parsley Pasta (p. 40)

Mandarin Spinach Salad (p. 62)

Le Colonel (p. 87)

▼

Salmon with Appeal

Ingredients:

1 5 oz. Salmon fillet

1 large Potato
(peeled into 10-1" x 5" strips)

3 teaspoons Butter

2 tablespoons Mayonnaise

Juice from 1/2 a Lime
(1 tablespoon max)

Instructions:

Melt butter in medium skillet. Lay potato strips on counter slightly overlapping and in two rows to make a 9" x 5" blanket of potatoes. Wrap salmon in the potatoes. The fish should be fully covered. Pick up the package and grill 5 minutes per side (until well browned.) Combine mayo and lime as side sauce.

Comments:

Ask for about 5 oz. of fresh salmon fillet. 5 oz. is about a 2" wide end of a full salmon fillet. The potato will stick easily to the fillet to allow you to fully cover the fish. Peel potato skin off first, then use the white part of potato for the recipe. Make sure the pan is at medium temperature to assure the fish cooks right and the butter doesn't burn. Apologies to Seattle for this crude (but delicious) recipe.

Nutritional Information:

	Salmon	Butter	Mayo	Potato
Fat 31.8 g	8.3	12.3	11	.2
Calories	125	111	99	110
Fat Percent	60%	100%	100%	2%

Serve with:

Rice with Chives (p. 48)

Feta Tomato Salad (p. 73)

Amaretto Strawberry (p. 86)

▼

Lamb Chops with Shallot

Ingredients:

3 1" thick Lamb Chops (Loin Chops)

1 cup fresh Parsley, chopped

1 Shallot, minced

Juice from 1/2 Lemon

2 tablespoons Butter

Instructions:

Broil lamb chops 3" from burners for 8 minutes. Meanwhile, blend remaining ingredients and set aside. After 8 minutes, turn chops over and broil 6 more minutes. After 6 minutes, top each chop with 1/3 of parsley mixture. Broil 1 minute and serve.

Comments:

These delicious chops are ready in just minutes. Note that half the fat is in the topping, so if you are watching fat, watch the topping! The best way to make the topping is in a food processor. Start the machine and drop in the peeled shallot, then the butter (cold), then the parsley and lemon.

Nutritional Information:

	Lamb (3)	Butter
Fat 48 g	24	24
Calories	540	216
Fat Percent	40%	100%

Serve with:

Parsley Pasta (p. 40)

Shrimp Cocktail (p. 69)

Le Colonel (p. 87)

Plant-Burger

Ingredients:

1 Eggplant*

**1/4 cup Italian Dressing
(eg; Paul Newman)**

1/4 cup Basil

2 tablespoons Oil

1 Roll

Instructions:

Brush all sides of eggplant with dressing (or soak for several minutes.) Meanwhile, blend the basil and oil in blender to form paste (or use store bought Pesto). Grill or broil the eggplant 4 minutes per side. Brush occasionally with more dressing. In the last minute top with 1 tablespoon of basil mix and brown bun for 30 seconds. Assemble sandwich and serve.

Comments:

*For one serving use a small Italian eggplant and slice lengthwise into six pieces. Serve on a hot dog bun. For multiple servings, like at a picnic, use the large eggplant and each serving should be a 1/2" slice from the eggplant (about hamburger size). Serve on hamburger bun. Also, add one slice cheese in the last minute of grilling if desired.

Nutritional Information:

	Eggplant	Dressing	Oil	Roll
Fat 21.6 g	.1	4.5	14	3
Calories	13	52	126	180
Fat Percent	7%	78%	100%	15%

Serve with:

Grilled Eggplant Chips (p. 56)

Garlic Shrimp Grill Skewers (p. 70)

Amaretto Strawberries (p. 86)

▼

Fajita

Ingredients:

**1/4 lb. Skirt Steak (4 oz),
trimmed of all fat**

2 tablespoons Worcestershire Sauce

1 tablespoon Butter

1 small Onion

2 Flour Tortillas

Instructions:

Place Worcestershire sauce and steak in a small dish to marinate together while preparing onion. Chop onion and place in small skillet with butter. Cook over medium heat until slightly brown. Grill steak four minutes per side. Slice cooked steak into small pieces along grain and divide between Flour Tortillas. Top with onion. Roll up and enjoy.

Comments:

Skirt steak is absolutely the best meat for fajita. If your grocer doesn't have it, you can substitute flank steak (cheaper) or a tenderloin (more expensive). Sliced avocados or sour cream also go well with Fajita, but increase the fat content of this meal.

Nutritional Information:

	Steak	Butter	Tortillas
Fat 25.3 g	8	12.3	5
Calories	193	111	118
Fat Percent	37%	100%	38%

Serve with:

Broiled Tomatoes (p. 35)

Good Salad (p. 74)

Baked Apple (p. 101)

▼

Garlic Chicken Puffs

Ingredients:

**1 Chicken Breast
(cut into 1 inch cubes)**

1 cup Pancake Mix

3/4 cup Milk

1/4 teaspoon Garlic Powder

2 tablespoons Oil

Instructions:

Heat oil in saucepan over high heat. Mix pancake mix, milk and garlic powder together. Dredge chicken cubes in batter & drop in hot oil. Fry until golden brown, about 1 minute each side. This recipe works best when the batter is chilled.

Comments:

Be extremely careful of splashing oil with this recipe. It is best to fry with a splash guard (a screen that goes over your pan to catch oil, but allows smoke out).

Nutritional Information:

	Chicken	Batter	Milk
Fat 13.6 g	6.1	1.5	6
Calories	179	450	112
Fat Percent	31%	3%	48%

Serve with:

Parsley Pasta (p. 40)

Stuffed Mushrooms (p. 75)

Blueberries and Cream (p. 94)

Coney Island Chili

Ingredients:

1/4 lb. lean Ground Beef

1/2 cup Onion, chopped (1 small onion)

3 tablespoons Tomato Paste

1/4 cup Water

1 teaspoon Chili Powder

Instructions:

"Saute" beef in saucepan over medium heat. Stir until beef is finely crumbled and browned, about 4 minutes. Add onions and cook about 1 minute. Add tomato, water and chili powder, continue to cook about 5 minutes over low heat.

Comments:

Adjust the flavor by adding more water (only 1 or 2 tablespoons) or more chili powder. There will be leftover tomato paste (sorry). Scoop tablespoon-sized heaps of tomato paste onto wax paper and freeze for future use.

Nutritional Information:

	Beef	Onion	Tomato
Fat 15.9 g	15.2	.2	.5
Calories	268	27	41
Fat Percent	51%	7%	11%

Serve with:

Beer Bread (p. 50)

Feta Tomato Salad (p. 73)

Le Colonel (p. 87)

Pesto Pasta

Ingredients:

1/4 cup Basil* (packed tight)

2 tablespoons Olive Oil

1 small Garlic Clove

2 tablespoons Parmesan Cheese

2 cups cooked Pasta

Instructions:

Blend first four ingredients into a paste. Toss with hot pasta. (2 Cups)

*Use spinach if basil is not available.

Comments:

Pesto is most easily made in a food processor. Start the machine and drop in the peeled garlic first. Follow with the basil, cheese and finally the oil.

Nutritional Information:

	Oil	Cheese
Fat 30.6 g	27.6	3
Calories	249	46
Fat Percent	100%	59%

Serve with:

Garlic Bread (p. 42)

Amaretto Strawberries (p. 86)

Teriyaki Chicken

Ingredients:

**2 small Chicken Breasts
(boneless/skinless)**

1/4 cup Teriyaki Sauce

Instructions:

Cut each breast lengthwise to form four strips about 2" x 6". Place chicken and sauce in plastic Ziplock™ type bag and marinate at least ten minutes. On hot barbecue or under broiler, grill chicken two minutes per side.

Comments:

Best barbecued over hot grill. Allow to burn slightly. Good as sandwich filler also.

Nutritional Information:

	Chicken
Fat 3.1 g	3.1
Calories	142
Fat Percent	20%

Serve with:

Broiled Tomatoes (p. 35)

Garlic Shrimp Grill Skewers (p. 70)

Amaretto Strawberries (p. 86)

Roast Garlic Chicken

Ingredients:

2 Chicken Breasts

1 head of Garlic, separated into cloves

1 teaspoon Olive Oil

1/2 cup White Wine

1 slice Wheat Bread, toasted

Instructions:

Heat oil in saucepan over medium high heat. Add chicken & garlic (unpeeled) except 1 clove. Saute 5 minutes, stirring garlic occasionally. Turn over chicken & continue sauteing 5 more minutes. Remove pan from heat, add wine, cover pan and cook on medium for 5 minutes. Rub toast with remaining clove. Serve chicken over toast with sauce.

Comments:

When cooked, the garlic will become soft and can be pressed out of its clove as a soft mellow spread that mixes deliciously with the sauce and chicken.

Nutritional Information:

	Chicken	Oil	Bread
Fat 8.1 g	3.1	4.6	.4
Calories	142	41.6	42
Fat Percent	20%	100%	9%

Serve with:

Broiled Tomatoes (p.35)

Mandarin Spinach Salad (p. 62)

Le Colonel (p. 87)

Little Foot Pizza

Ingredients:

One 14.5 oz. can Whole Tomatoes, chopped well

11 oz. Breadstick Dough*

2 tablespoons Flour

4 oz. Mozzarella, shredded

4 teaspoons Oregano

Instructions:

Preheat oven to 500°. Place the rack on the lowest position. On the counter top, carefully open the breadstick package. Take three round segments of dough (two for thin pizza) and keeping them stacked press them down to start forming the pizza dough. Sprinkle the counter and dough with flour to remove the stickiness. Using a rolling pin, roll out the dough to 8" in diameter. Top with 3 tablespoons of tomato, 1 teaspoon oregano and 1/4 of the cheese (in that order). Place on cookie sheet and cook 7 minutes (edges will brown). Repeat to make 2 additional pies!

Comments:

*This dough is found in the refrigerated section of the grocer, near the cheese and dairy. You can use any of the brands that are intended for making biscuits or rolls or bread. This is an excellent basic pizza that tastes like real pizza—unlike most recipes for home pizza. This recipe will make 3 or 4 pizzas. Nutrition information is for 1 pizza.

Nutritional Information:

	Tomato	Dough	Cheese
Fat 9.5 g	0	5	4.5
Calories	15	220	72
Fat Percent	0%	20%	56%

Serve with:

Garlic Bread (p. 42)

Good Salad (p. 74)

Amaretto Strawberries (p. 86)

▼

Beef in Wok

Ingredients:

1/4 lb. Flank Steak, sliced thin

1 teaspoon Soy Sauce

2 teaspoons Flour

1 tablespoon Oil

12 Snow Peas, trimmed and cut in half

Instructions:

Slice the flank steak into small pieces across the grain with a sharp knife. Place in a Ziplock™. bag with the soy sauce and flour and toss well until meat is coated. Heat oil in a medium skillet over high heat. Have about 1/4 cup of water at hand. When oil is hot add meat, mix and sauté for about two minutes until cooked. As meat cooks and flour starts to stick to bottom of pan, "deglaze" with water. This will form a gravy. Use only as much water as needed to form a little gravy. After 2 minutes add snow peas and toss for about 30 more seconds.

Comments:

There are a lot of flavored soy sauces on the market for making stir fry dishes. They are all good for this recipe as well. Notice that this stir fry is done using a flat pan. Many Chinese cooks use flat pans instead of woks.

Nutritional Information:

	Steak	Oil
Fat	22 g	8	14
Calories	193	125
Fat Percent	37%	100%

Serve with:

Rice with Chives (p. 48)

Pot Stickers (p. 67)

Apple Compote (p. 97)

▼

Orange Roughy

Ingredients:

1 Orange Roughy Fillet (about 6 oz.)

2 tablespoons Creamy Italian Salad Dressing

1/2 Lemon

Instructions:

Preheat the oven on broil setting and arrange the broiling pan so that the fish will be about 5″ below the broiler elements. Cover the pan with a large piece of aluminum foil. Place the fillet on the aluminum foil in the pan. Spread the dressing over the entire fillet. Broil 10 minutes without turning fish over.

Comments:

The fillet should not be thicker than one inch at any point or it will not cook all the way through.

Nutritional Information:

	Roughy	Dressing
Fat 23 g	14	9
Calories	248	104
Fat Percent	51%	78%

Serve with:

Peas & Red Pepper (p. 43)

French Onion Soup (p. 61)

Le Colonel (p. 87)

Fettuccine Alfredo

Ingredients:

1 tablespoon Butter

1 tablespoon Flour

1/2 cup Milk

1/4 cup Parmesan Cheese

1 cup Fettuccine, cooked and drained

Instructions:

In a saucepan over medium heat, combine the butter and flour for one minute (stirring constantly). It will form a paste. Add the milk and stir for 2 minutes. The mixture will thicken slightly. Add the grated (fresh) Parmesan cheese and stir 30 seconds. Remove from heat. Add pasta and toss with sauce. Additionally you can place the plate (if ovenproof) under the broiler for 3 minutes to add a brownish crust to the top.

Comments:

The flour and butter combined forms a roux, a basic element of many French recipes. Also, when the milk is added and a sauce is formed this white sauce is used as the base for many popular sauces. This meal is high fat, but cooks up in 7 minutes. Skim milk will work and cut the fat slightly.

Nutritional Information:

	Butter	Milk	Cheese	Pasta
Fat 15.3 g	12.3	.5	1.5	1
Calories	111	9.3	23	159
Fat Percent	100%	48%	59%	6%

Serve with:

Garlic Bread (p. 42)

Mandarin Spinach Salad (p. 62)

Amaretto Strawberries (p. 86)

Sea Bass à Teriyaki

Ingredients:

1 6 oz. Sea Bass Fillet

1/4 cup Teriyaki Sauce

2 Green Onions (scallions)

Instructions:

Place the fillet and teriyaki sauce in a Ziplock™ plastic bag and set aside for five minutes to marinate. Set the oven to broil and arrange the broiling pan so that the fish will be about 5" below the broiler elements. Cover the pan with a large piece of aluminum foil. Take fillet out of marinade and place on the aluminum foil in the pan. Broil 4 minutes per side, and brush with extra sauce after turning. Top with sliced green onions.

Comments:

Use only the white part of the green onion. This is the only part that is really edible or has flavor. It's best to remove the tassel and slice the white part into thin disks.

Nutritional Information:

	Sea Bass
Fat 5.2 g	5.2
Calories	208
Fat Percent	23%

Serve with:

Honey Beans (p. 39)

French Onion Soup (p. 61)

Amaretto Strawberries (p. 86)

Tuna Steak

Ingredients:

1 Tuna Steak* (1″ thick)

1 Lemon

Instructions:

Set the oven to broil and arrange the broiling pan so that the steak will be about 5″ below the broiler elements. Cover the pan with a large piece of aluminum foil. Place steak on the aluminum foil in the pan. Squeeze the juice from 1/2 the lemon over the steak. Broil 4 minutes per side, and squeeze the other half of the lemon over the steak after turning.

Comments:

You may want to top the tuna with a little dill or parsley to add color to the fish. With the lemon juice, the fish may look bland, but if it is not overcooked it will be delicious.

*Yellowfin Tuna - 6 oz

Nutritional Information:

	Tuna
Fat 10.8 g	10.8
Calories	274
Fat Percent	35%

Serve with:

Honey Beans (p. 39)

Good Salad (p. 74)

Chocolate Soufflé (p. 84)

▼

Macaroni & Cheese

Ingredients:

1 tablespoon Butter

1 tablespoon Flour

1/2 cup Milk

1/2 cup Sharp Cheddar Cheese, grated

3/4 cup Elbow Macaroni

Instructions:

In a saucepan over medium heat, combine the butter and flour for one minute (stirring constantly). It will form a paste. Add the milk and stir for 2 minutes (or until it starts to thicken). Add the grated cheese and stir 30 seconds. Remove from heat. Add pasta and toss the sauce. Transfer to an oven proof serving dish. Now broil for 3 minutes to add a brownish crust to the top.

Comments:

Notice the similarity between this recipe and the Alfredo recipe. Again the basic white sauce is the base of the sauce.

Nutritional Information:

	Butter	Milk	Cheese	Pasta
Fat 16.8 g	12.3	.5	3	1
Calories	111	9.3	46	159
Fat Percent	100%	48%	59%	6%

Serve with:

Garlic Bread (p. 42)

Good Salad (p. 74)

Kahlua Vanilla Nuts (p. 92)

▼

Veal Mushrooms and Wine

Ingredients:

1 Veal Cutlet Scaloppini

4 Mushrooms, sliced

1 teaspoon Olive Oil

1/4 cup Dry White Wine

2 teaspoons Lemon Juice

Instructions:

Heat oil in small saucepan over medium heat. Saute mushrooms then add veal to pan for 1-1/2 minutes per side; 3 minutes total. Remove to plate. Remove pan from heat. Add wine and lemon juice. Heat slowly two minutes or until liquid is thickened. Pour over veal.

Comments:

1 clove garlic can be substituted for lemon juice.

Nutritional Information:

	Veal	Oil
Fat 17.1 g	12.5	4.6
Calories	246	41.6
Fat Percent	46%	100%

Serve with:

Broiled Tomatoes (p. 35)

Good Salad (p. 74)

Le Colonel (p. 87)

Steak Diane

Ingredients:

One 2" Tenderloin (5 oz. Fillet Mignon)

1 tablespoon Olive Oil

1 Shallot, minced

2 tablespoons Worcestershire Sauce

2 tablespoons Sherry

Instructions:

Slice tenderloin crossways into two 1" rounds. Heat oil in saucepan over high heat and cook steaks for 1 minute per side. (This will smoke the kitchen!) Remove steaks from pan. Turn heat to medium. Take pan off burner and sauté minced shallot in hot pan for one minute. Return pan to stove and add steaks, sauce & sherry. Stir for 3 minutes. Transfer steaks to a plate, cover with sauce and serve.

Comments:

If you allow yourself to enjoy red meat only occasionally, do it right! This is absolutely delicious! The best meal you can have for about $5. For extra razzle dazzle, add 1 tablespoon of Cognac before sauce & sherry and ignite it with a match. Continue with recipe when flames die down.

Nutritional Information:

	Steak	Olive Oil
Fat 16 g	6.8	9.2
Calories	232	83
Fat Percent	26%	100%

Serve with:

Zoom Shrooms (p. 38)

Mandarin Spinach Salad (p. 62)

Le Colonel (p. 87)

▼

Mom's Hamburgers

Ingredients:

1/4 lbs. regular Ground Beef

2 teaspoons Butter

2 tablespoons Vermouth

Instructions:

Form the meat into a hamburger patty about 3 1/2" wide by 1/2" thick. (Most people make their hamburgers too thick and it doesn't cook right.) Over medium heat, in a small frying pan, cook the patty for about 3 minutes per side (less if you like it a little rare). Remove patty to a plate and "deglaze" the pan with the butter and vermouth. Pour sauce over patty on a large plate.

Comments:

When your mother is French and Jewish this is what you get when you ask for a hamburger. Remember, when shopping for one serving, to ask the meat department to package a quarter pound for you, so there is no leftover.

Notice that vermouth is an inexpensive cooking liquid that's great to have on hand.

Nutritional Information:

	Beef	Butter
Fat 12.2 g	4	8.2
Calories	50	74
Fat Percent	72%	100%

Serve with:

Zoom Shrooms (p. 38)

Good Salad (p. 74)

Kahlua Vanilla Nuts (p. 92)

▼

Spaghetti with Mussels

Ingredients:

12 Mussels

One 14.5 oz. can Stewed Tomatoes

2 cups Spaghetti, cooked

Instructions:

Cook spaghetti. Rinse mussels under cold water and pull off any stringy attachments. (Good mussels should be clean and the shells closed). Add mussels and stewed tomatoes to small saucepan and cover. Mussels will not be fully submerged and don't have to be because they will cook by "steaming." Cook on high until liquid boils then change to low heat and cook for six minutes. Put finished spaghetti on serving plate. Dump mussels and tomatoes on top of spaghetti. Discard any mussels that haven't opened. (These are not edible.)

Comments:

Some canned stewed tomatoes now come with herbs added, such as basil and garlic. These are excellent substitutes for the plain stewed tomatoes.

Nutritional Information:

	Mussels	Tomatoes	Spaghetti
Fat 4.2 g	2.2	0	2
Calories	95	105	318
Fat Percent	21%	0%	6%

Serve with:

Garlic Bread (p. 42)

Mandarin Spinach Salad (p. 62)

Le Colonel (p. 87)

The Breaded Salmon

Ingredients:

1 6 oz. Salmon Fillet (about 1/3 lb.)

2 tablespoons Mayonnaise

1 teaspoon Mustard

1/4 cup Italian Bread Crumbs

Instructions:

Preheat oven to 350°. Check salmon for small white bones and remove any. Place fillet in a baking dish, with skin side down. Mix mayonnaise and mustard together and spread evenly over salmon. Press bread crumbs onto salmon. Dump excess crumbs out. Bake for 18 minutes.

Comments:

Be sure to get a fillet (not a salmon steak). When cooked salmon will be evenly pale all the way through. Make additional mustard/mayo mix as a side sauce for the cooked fish.

Nutritional Information:

	Salmon	Mayo	Bread crumbs
Fat 31.5 g	8.3	22	1.2
Calories	125	198	98
Fat Percent	60%	100%	11%

Serve with:

Rice with Chives (p. 48)

Feta Tomato Salad (p. 73)

Amaretto Strawberries (p. 86)

Scallops Toronado Bundles

Ingredients:

8 large Sea Scallops

1 Scallion

2 teaspoons Butter

1/2 package Chinese Noodles (Ramen)

1/2 cup Water

Instructions:

Bring large pot of water to boil. Add Chinese noodles; cook 4 minutes. Remove noodles, reserving hot liquid, and set noodles aside. Soften scallions in the reserved water for 30 seconds, then tear off two long strips. (Fibers of scallion will tear lengthwise easily.) Melt butter in small skillet over medium heat. Place four scallops side by side in a square and tie together with one of the long strips of scallion. Repeat with remaining four scallops. Lift scallop bundle with spatula and place in skillet carefully, 2 minutes per side. Remove, and add water and noodles.

"Deglaze" pan with water and noodles until pan is dry. Place noodles on plate and top with the two scallop bundles.

Comments:

This is a very attractive presentation that takes a little practice to get right. The first time the packages may fall apart. Don't worry. With practice you will be able to cook the noodles in the 1/2 cup of water while "deglazing" instead of cooking them ahead.

Nutritional Information:

	Scallops	Butter	Ramen
Fat 15.1 g	2.8	8.3	4
Calories	224	75	80
Fat Percent	11%	100%	45%

Serve with:

Flavored Rice (p. 55)

Ebi (p. 80)

Apple Compote (p. 97)

▼

Shrimp Scampi

Ingredients:

1/2 lb. Shrimp (8 large or 12 medium)

1 tablespoon Butter

2 cloves Garlic, crushed

1/4 teaspoon Oregano

2 tablespoons Sherry, White Wine or Lemon

Instructions:

Wash and peel shrimp. Melt butter in medium skillet over medium heat; add garlic. Arrange shrimp in skillet in a single layer. Cook shrimp 2 1/2 minutes until fully pink. Turn each shrimp over and cook an additional 2 1/2 minutes. Add oregano and sherry and "deglaze" the pan with the sherry. Remove shrimp to serving plate and cover with the sauce.

Comments:

This is the author's favorite "no-brainer" dinner. For even quicker and easier preparation, you can use cooked shrimp. In this case, cook the shrimp only 1 to 2 minutes per side, since they've already been cooked. You may also choose to substitute olive oil or half oil/half butter for the butter in the recipe, for a different flavor.

Nutritional Information:

	Shrimp	Butter
Fat 15.9 g	3.6	12.3
Calories	182	111
Fat Percent	18%	100%

Serve with:

Rice with Chives (p. 48)

Good Salad (p. 74)

Le Colonel (p. 87)

Scallops in Wine Sauce

Ingredients:

1/4 lb. small Scallops (Calico Scallops)

1 tablespoon Butter

2 tablespoons Basil (4 big leaves), chopped

2 tablespoons White Wine

Instructions:

Melt butter in medium skillet over medium heat. Add scallops and basil; sauté 5 minutes or until scallops are completely opaque and starting to brown. Add wine and sauté another minute. Remove from heat and serve immediately.

Comments:

White wine sold in small 8 fl. oz. bottles is perfect for this recipe. It gives you enough for the recipe and just enough to serve with the meal. No waste!

Nutritional Information:

	Scallops	Butter
Fat 13.5 g	1.2	12.3
Calories	81	111
Fat Percent	13%	100%

Serve with:

Garlic & Oil Angel Pasta (p. 44)

Good Salad (p. 74)

Le Colonel (p. 87)

▼

Breaded Veal

Ingredients:

**1/4 lb. Veal Scaloppini
(thin Veal Cutlet)**

1 Egg

1/4 cup Italian Bread Crumbs

1 tablespoon Butter

1 Lemon

Instructions:

Beat egg and pour out onto a plate. On a second plate, spread out the bread crumbs. Dredge both sides of the veal scaloppini (or scaloppines if you have several small pieces) in the egg. Place veal on the plate with the bread crumbs, and turn over to coat both sides. Heat butter in medium skillet over medium heat. When melted, add veal, taking care not to overlap pieces, and cook 2 minutes per side. Remove to plate. Squeeze the juice from half a lemon over scaloppines.

Comments:

The egg and crumb breading in this recipe is a basic technique found in many recipes. You can change this recipe by adding different spices to the bread crumbs. Note also that all the butter and egg for this recipe doesn't find its way into the final dish, and the nutritional information has been adjusted accordingly.

Nutritional Information:

	Veal	Egg	Butter	Bread
Fat 18.1 g	6	2.8	8.1	1.2
Calories	204	31	73	98
Fat Percent	26%	81%	100%	11%

Serve with:

Honey Beans (p. 39)

Feta Tomato Salad (p. 73)

Grand Marnier Oranges (p. 90)

▼

Grilled Pizza

Ingredients:

1 11 oz. package Breadstick Dough

2 tablespoons Flour

3 oz. Feta Cheese, crumbled

4 oz. small Cooked Shrimp

2 tablespoons Vegetable Oil

Instructions:

Prepare grill, allowing coals to burn down white so that no flame remains. Generously flour countertop and carefully open the breadstick package. Take three round segments of dough (two for thin pizza) and, keeping them stacked, press them down to start forming the pizza crust. (If the dough is too sticky to handle, sprinkle with more flour.) Using a rolling pin, roll out the dough to 8" in diameter. Brush both sides with a little oil. Place dough on barbeque grill (yes, really) and grill one minute until dough browns; be careful not to allow it to burn!

Flip over and top with feta cheese and shrimp. Remove after one minute and serve.

Comments:

Yes, this really does go on the barbeque grill. Only two things can go wrong: the dough can burn if you don't watch it, or it can puff up if the coals are not hot enough. If it puffs, pierce to deflate and continue to grill until browned.

This pizza may also be prepared in your broiler.

Nutritional Information:

	Feta	Dough	Shrimp	Oil
Fat 38.8 g	18	5	1.8	14
Calories	225	220	91	126
Fat Percent	72%	20%	18%	100%

Serve with:

Good Salad (p. 74)

Amaretto Strawberries (p. 86)

Fried Rice

Ingredients:

1 cup cooked Rice

2 teaspoons Oil

1/4 cup Onion, minced (small onion)

2 teaspoons Soy Sauce

1 Egg, well-beaten

Instructions:

Cook rice by boiling 10 minutes in water (or use Minute Rice™). Saute minced onions in oil, in a small saucepan for 5 minutes or until browned. Add cooked rice and soy sauce and stir about 30 seconds. Add well beaten egg, and remove pan from stove. Mix well, until mixture is just dry and rice grains are separate.

Comments:

Fried rice is a good place to dump tidbits of leftover shrimp, scallop, scallion and green onion. Add the seafood, cut in small pieces, to the onion; add the greens after the onions are translucent.

Nutritional Information:

	Rice	Oil	Egg
Fat 20.4 g	2.4	12.4	5.6
Calories	222	112	63
Fat Percent	10%	100%	80%

Serve with:

Veal Piccata (p. 4)

Teriyaki Chicken (p. 13)

Sea Bass á Teriyaki (p. 19)

Side Dishes

▼

Sesame Broccoli

Ingredients:

1 cup Broccoli Florets

1 tablespoon Sesame Seeds

2 teaspoons Honey

1 tablespoon Soy Sauce

Instructions:

Cook broccoli by "steaming" over boiling water. "Steam" for 3 minutes; broccoli will turn a bright green. Remove from heat; allow to cool to room temperature for easier handling. Toss with remaining ingredients.

Comments:

Remember to get the broccoli florets from salad bars rather than buying a whole broccoli (see "Shopping Strategies" on page 106).

Nutritional Information:

	Broccoli	Honey
Fat	.4 g	.4	0
Calories	12	42
Fat Percent	30%	0%

Serve with:

Lemon Chicken (p. 2)

Parsley Pasta (p. 40)

Chocolate Soufflé (p. 84)

▼

Broiled Tomatoes

Ingredients:

1 Tomato

1 tablespoon Butter

1 small French Roll, crumbled

1 teaspoon Rosemary

Instructions:

Set oven to broil. Slice tomato in half and place cut side up in an oven-proof dish. Blend together butter, crumbled roll, and rosemary, and spoon mixture onto tomatoes. Broil 4" from the broiler elements for 3 minutes.

Comments:

This is a great side dish whenever you are broiling.

Nutritional Information:

	Tomato	Butter	Roll
Fat 13 g	.3	12.3	.4
Calories	24	111	137
Fat Percent	11%	100%	3%

Serve with:

Lemon Chicken (p. 2)

Teriyaki Chicken (p. 13)

Roast Garlic Chicken (p. 14)

▼

Dijon Pasta

Ingredients:

2 cups Pasta

2 tablespoons Butter

1 tablespoon Dijon Mustard

1 teaspoon Parsley

Instructions:

Mash together butter, Dijon mustard and parsley. Cook pasta, drain and return to pan. Toss butter mixture and hot pasta until well-coated.

Comments:

Don't try to force all the butter mixture to melt; when the pasta is coated, discard excess mixture. Serve immediately because the butter and Dijon mustard tend to separate if allowed to sit too long.

Nutritional Information:

	Pasta	Butter
Fat 26.6 g	2.6	24
Calories	560	216
Fat Percent	4%	100%

Serve with:

Lemon Chicken (p. 2)

Roast Garlic Chicken (p. 14)

Veal Mushrooms and Wine (p. 22)

Side Dishes

▼

Sweet Potato Side

Ingredients:

1 medium Sweet Potato*

2 tablespoons Milk

1/4 teaspoon Cinnamon

1/2 cup Miniature Marshmallows **

Instructions:

Microwave sweet potato 6 minutes. Cut in half (careful, it will be hot) and scoop soft inside from potato (about 1/2 cup). Mash together with milk and cinnamon until well-mixed. Spoon mixture into an oven-proof cup (such as a ramekin) and smooth mixture. Press marshmallows over the top of mixture. Broil 1 minute until browned and serve.

Comments:

*Use the vegetable scale at the supermarket to find a half-pound sweet potato.

**Notice that marshmallows, although full of sugar, have no fat.

Nutritional Information:

	Potato	Milk	Marshmallow
Fat .55 g	.5	.05	0
Calories	172	10.5	50
Fat Percent	3%	4%	0%

Serve with:

Lemon Chicken (p. 2)

Teriyaki Chicken (p. 13)

Veal Mushrooms and Wine (p. 22)

▼

Zoom Shrooms

Ingredients:

1 cup fresh Mushrooms (6 medium)

1 teaspoon Olive Oil

1 clove Garlic, pressed

Fresh ground Pepper

Instructions:

Cut stem of mushrooms short, and slice mushrooms into quarters. Heat oil in medium skillet. Sauté all ingredients over medium heat for 3 minutes. Serve.

Comments:

Note: If desired, 1/4 teaspoon of garlic powder can be substituted for the clove of garlic.

Nutritional Information:

	Mushroom	Oil
Fat 4.4 g	.2	4.2
Calories	9	38
Fat Percent	20%	100%

Serve with:

Lamb Chops with Shallots (p. 7)

Steak Diane (p. 23)

Mom's Hamburgers (p. 24)

Honey Beans

Ingredients:

12 fresh String Beans

1 tablespoon Honey

Instructions:

Cut or break off both ends of each bean (about 1/4" off each end). Place beans in pot with enough water to cover them. Heat to boiling and cook an additional 3 minutes on low heat; remove pan from heat. Drain, and add honey to the beans. Toss until honey forms a glaze over beans. Serve.

Comments:

Green beans or string beans are best eaten a little on the crunchy side, so take care not to overcook them or they will be mushy. This recipe also demonstrates how easy it is to cut down on fats by substituting other flavors like honey.

Nutritional Information:

	Beans	Honey
Fat 0 g	0	0
Calories	2	64
Fat Percent	0%	0%

Serve with:

Lemon Chicken (p. 2)

Veal Piccata (p. 4)

Teriyaki Chicken (p. 13)

Parsley Pasta

Ingredients:

1 cup cooked Egg Noodles

1 teaspoon Butter

1/2 teaspoon Parsley Flakes

Instructions:

Cook egg noodles in large pot for 5 minutes or as directed on package. Drain in colander (spaghetti strainer), rinsing in hot water. Shake dry. Melt butter in the hot empty pot you used to cook the noodles. Add hot pasta and parsley flakes and toss gently.

Comments:

Pasta is a great side dish for most meals. See the section on "Techniques" (p. 110) for how to keep and reheat pasta for even quicker preparations.

Nutritional Information:

	Noodles	Butter
Fat 6.6 g	2.5	4.1
Calories	210	37
Fat Percent	11%	100%

Serve with:

Lemon Chicken (p. 2)

Lamb Chops with Shallot (p. 7)

Roast Garlic Chicken (p. 14)

Mushroom Onion Side

Ingredients:

1/4 cup Mushrooms, sliced

1/4 cup Onions, sliced

1 teaspoon Vegetable Oil

Pepper

Instructions:

Combine and sauté ingredients over medium heat for 7 minutes. Onions should be translucent and mushrooms should be browned slightly.

Comments:

This recipe is great with all meat dishes and a real "no-brainer" if you get all ingredients from the salad bar. Put them all in a salad bar container and when it's time for dinner, dump them into a medium skillet and cook.

Nutritional Information:

	Oil
Fat 4.6 g	4.6
Calories	41.6
Fat Percent	100%

Serve with:

Roast Garlic Chicken (p. 14)

Orange Roughy (p. 17)

Steak Diane (p. 23)

Garlic Bread

Ingredients:

1 small French Roll, split in half

2 tablespoons Butter

1 clove Shallot, minced

2 cloves Garlic, minced

1 teaspoon Olive Oil

Instructions:

Melt the butter and combine with the shallot, garlic and oil. Spread the mixture evenly over the face of each of the halves of the split French roll. Cover to the edges or they will burn when browning. Place bread face up in broiler 4" from the elements and broil 4 minutes until browned. Cut each half into 4 slices.

Comments:

The timing on this recipe seems to vary considerably. Watch the bread while it's under the broiler to make sure it does not burn. If you have pesto from another recipe, you can use 2 tablespoons of that instead of the garlic, shallots and oil.

Nutritional Information:

	Roll	Butter	Oil
Fat 29.8 g	.4	24.6	4.8
Calories	137	221	43
Fat Percent	3%	100%	100%

Serve with:

Pasta Quick (p. 3)

Pesto Pasta (p. 12)

Fettuccine Alfredo (p. 18)

Peas & Red Pepper

Ingredients:

1/4 cup Peas

1 tablespoon Red Bell Pepper*

Instructions:

Using a sharp knife, cube the red pepper into small squares slightly larger than the peas. Toss together with the peas and serve cold, or "blanch" the peas and peppers by lowering them into boiling water for 30 seconds. Peas can also be steamed for about 30 seconds.

Comments:

This is the perfect vegetable dish; peas and peppers are both extremely good sources of fiber and have no fat. They can usually be found at the salad bar. Otherwise use frozen or canned peas.

* Red pepper is a vegetable, not a spice.

Nutritional Information:

	Peas	Pepper
Fat 0 g	0	0
Calories	25	3
Fat Percent	0%	0%

Serve with:

Lemon Chicken (p. 2)

Veal Piccata (p. 4)

Roast Garlic Chicken (p. 14)

Garlic & Oil Angel Pasta

Ingredients:

1 cup Angel Hair Pasta (about 1 oz.)

1 teaspoon Olive Oil

1 clove Garlic

Instructions:

Cook pasta in boiling water for 2 minutes; be careful not to overcook. Drain into a colander and rinse in warm to hot water. (This step prevents the angel hair from clumping together due to loose flour on the pasta's strands.) Shake lightly to remove excess water. Heat oil in the empty pan. When hot, remove from stove and sauté the crushed garlic in the oil. After 30 seconds remove the larger pieces of garlic, add the pasta, and toss. Serve on warm plate.

Comments:

This cooks up in only 2 minutes, and is a great side dish for a wide variety of main courses.

Nutritional Information:

	Pasta	Oil
Fat	5.3 g	1	4.8
Calories	159	43
Fat Percent	6%	100%

Serve with:

Teriyaki Chicken (p. 13)

Veal Mushrooms and Wine (p. 22)

Steak Diane (p. 23)

Peas in Zucchini Cups

Ingredients:

1 medium Zucchini

1/4 cup Peas

1/4 teaspoon Dill, chopped

Instructions:

Boil a large pot of water. Using a potato peeler, make stripes an inch or so apart down the whole length of the zucchini. (This is for visual appeal only). Cut both ends off the zucchini and then slice it into three even pieces, so you have three chunks of zucchini about 3" high. Scoop out the inside of each chunk with a small spoon or a melon-baller to form three little cups. (Make sure the walls and bottom of the cups are at least 1/4" thick.) Drop the zucchini cups in boiling water for 3 minutes. Meanwhile, mix peas and dill. Remove zucchini cups carefully from water and drain. Fill each with one-third of pea mixture and serve.

Comments:

These zucchini cups are a small side dish but they are a very attractive presentation for guests. Peas are usually available at the salad bar.

Nutritional Information:

	Zuchinni	Peas
Fat	.3 g .2	.1
Calories	28	33
Fat Percent	6%	3%

Serve with:

Salmon with Appeal (p. 6)

Teriyaki Chicken (p. 13)

Shrimp Scampi (p. 28)

▼

Sour Cream Mushrooms

Ingredients:

9 Mushrooms (sliced)

1 tablespoon Butter

2 tablespoons Sour Cream

Instructions:

Melt the butter in a medium skillet over medium heat. When melted, add mushrooms and sauté until softened, about 7 minutes. Remove pan from stove and stir in the sour cream completely covering the mushrooms. (Do not heat the sour cream on the stove.) Serve.

Comments:

Nine mushrooms is about 1/4 pound. Again, the salad bar at your supermarket will have sliced, washed mushrooms ready to cook. Many will also have sour cream.

Nutritional Information:

	Butter	Sour Cream
Fat 14.8 g	12.3	2.5
Calories	111	30
Fat Percent	100%	75%

Serve with:

Lamb Chops with Shallot (p. 7)

Fajita (p. 9)

Teriyaki Chicken (p. 13)

▼

Soy & Sesame Bean Sprouts

Ingredients:

1 cup fresh Bean Sprouts

1 teaspoon Butter

1 tablespoon Soy Sauce

1/2 teaspoon Sesame Seeds

Instructions:

Melt butter with bean sprouts in a skillet over medium heat for 5 minutes, or until the sprouts shrink and begin to curl up. Do not overcook or they will dry out. Add sesame seeds after 4 minutes of cooking time. Remove from heat and stir in soy sauce. Serve.

Comments:

Fresh bean sprouts will be white and crisp when snapped. A brownish or bruised appearance indicates that they are not fresh.

Nutritional Information:

	Butter
Fat 4.1 g	4.1
Calories	37
Fat Percent	100%

Serve with:

Teriyaki Chicken (p. 13)

Beef in Wok (p. 16)

Fried Rice (p. 32)

▼

Rice with Chives

Ingredients:

1/2 cup Rice

1 tablespoon Chives, chopped finely

Instructions:

"Quick cook" the rice. In a large pot of boiling water, boil the rice for 10 minutes, stirring occasionally to prevent sticking (just like pasta). After 10 minutes drain the rice and toss with chopped chives. Serve.

Comments:

This is a great quick-cooking technique for rice. You can also use green or fried onions in place of the chives.

Nutritional Information:

	Rice
Fat 1.2g	1.2
Calories	111
Fat Percent	10%

Serve with:

Orange Roughy (p. 17)

Scallops Toronado (p. 27)

Shrimp Scampi (p. 28)

▼

Fresh Asparagus

Ingredients:

6 stalks fresh Asparagus

1 tablespoon Butter (cut in small bits)

1/2 teaspoon Sesame Seeds

Instructions:

Cut off the tough end of the asparagus at an angle. Lay stalks flat at the bottom of a skillet. (Trim more off the back of the stalk if needed so they will lay flat.) Add just enough water to cover the asparagus. Heat pan and boil asparagus for 3 minutes. Drain pan; remove asparagus to serving dish and top with butter. Add sesame seeds to empty pot and toast them until slightly brown (2 minutes). Sprinkle over asparagus.

Comments:

For a real no-fat version of this, replace the butter with soy sauce. If you are watching your sodium intake, low-sodium soy sauce is available.

Nutritional Information:

	Butter
Fat 12.4 g	12.4
Calories	112
Fat Percent	100%

Serve with:

Lemon Chicken (p. 2)

Fettuccine Alfredo (p. 18)

Veal Mushrooms and Wine (p. 22)

Beer Bread

Ingredients:

1 cup self-rising Flour

1/3 cup Beer

1 tablespoon Sugar

1 Egg, well beaten

Instructions:

Preheat oven to 400°. Mix the flour, sugar and beer in a bowl, forming a dough. If the dough is a little sticky, add 1 tablespoon of flour at a time until the dough is smooth. Shape dough into a small loaf or two rolls and place on a cookie sheet. Brush a little egg on the top of the loaf to help it brown. Cook 20 minutes; cooked bread will sound hollow when tapped.

Comments:

This recipe forms a kind of heavy bread that is almost like a biscuit. It's included here more for its novelty as well as its taste.

Self-rising flour can be found in bulk foods.

Nutritional Information:

	Flour	Beer	Sugar
Fat 1.2 g	1.2	0	0
Calories	436	49	46
Fat Percent	2%	0%	0%

Serve with:

Lamb Chops with Shallot (p. 7)

Roast Garlic Chicken (p. 14)

Beef in Wok (p.16)

Noodles & Gravy

Ingredients:

1/2 Bouillon Cube, beef or chicken

1/2 cup Water

1 teaspoon Flour

1 cup Egg Noodles, cooked

Instructions:

Place bouillon cube and water in a small skillet over medium heat, and stir until dissolved. Allow mixture to come to a boil for about 15 seconds and remove from heat. Add flour slowly, stirring as mixture thickens into a gravy. Add noodles and toss to coat.

Comments:

Vermouth can be substituted for half of the water. To prevent lumps in the gravy, add the flour a third at a time, stirring continuously to mix, until gravy reaches desired thickness.

Nutritional Information:

	Noodles	Flour
Fat 3.62 g	3.6	.02
Calories	300	9
Fat Percent	11%	2%

Serve with:

Lamb Chops with Shallot (p. 7)

Teriyaki Chicken (p. 13)

Roast Garlic Chicken (p. 14)

Side Dishes ▼

▼

Tofu Stir Fry

Ingredients:

1/4 cup Tofu (2 oz. or four 1" cubes from salad bar)

1 Scallion (cut in 1/2" pieces)

1 teaspoon Vegetable Oil

1 teaspoon Soy Sauce

Instructions:

Cut tofu into 1/2" x 1/2" cubes. Heat oil in small non-stick fry pan on high heat. When oil is hot, stir in scallion for 30 seconds, stirring occasionally. Add tofu cubes and stir occasionally for about 2 minutes until tofu has browned slightly. (Tofu is fragile, so stir carefully.) Remove from heat, add soy sauce, stir quickly again, and serve.

Comments:

Scallions (a member of the onion family) are sometimes known as green onions. This recipe uses the whole scallion, unlike most recipes which only use the white part; cut off just the tassel on one end. Tofu (soybean curd) is found in the vegetable section of your supermarket.

Nutritional Information:

	Tofu	Oil
Fat 7.3 g	2.7	4.8
Calories	43	43
Fat Percent	57%	100%

Serve with:

Lemon Chicken (p. 2)

Beef in Wok (p. 16)

Fried Rice (p. 32)

Lemon Spinach

Ingredients:

1 cup fresh Spinach

1 teaspoon Lemon Juice

1/8 teaspoon Pepper

1/2 teaspoon Sesame Seeds

Instructions:

Wash spinach leaves (about 6 large leaves). Place wet spinach in small saucepan and cover. Cook over medium heat for about 5 minutes until leaves wilt. Add sesame seeds. Remove pan from heat and squeeze in about 2 teaspoons lemon juice. Grind a little fresh pepper over spinach and serve.

Comments:

This is a no-fat side dish that is easy to make while other things are cooking. Be light on the lemon juice because even a little too much will make the dish unpleasant.

Nutritional Information:

	Spinach
Fat .2 g	.2
Calories	12
Fat Percent	15%

Serve with:

Lamb Chops with Shallot (p. 7)

Roast Garlic Chicken (p. 14)

Beef in Wok (p. 16)

String Bean Bundles

Ingredients:

12 fresh String Beans

1 Scallion

1 Lemon

Instructions:

Place small pot of water on stove and add scallion. Meanwhile, snap off both ends of each string bean. When water boils, remove green onions and peel off two long pieces of scallion. Using wet scallions snugly tie the beans in two bundles of six each. Trim off extra scallion. Drop both packages into boiling water for 4 minutes. Remove and place on serving plates. Top with a squeeze of lemon.

Comments:

This is another very attractive and simple side dish. Lift the packages out carefully with a spatula so as not to damage them.

Nutritional Information:

	Beans
Fat .1 g	.1
Calories	22
Fat Percent	4%

Serve with:

Lemon Chicken (p. 2)

Salmon with Appeal (p. 6)

Scallops Toronado (p. 27)

Flavored Rice

Ingredients:

1/2 cup Rice

1 10.5 oz can Chicken Broth

Instructions:

Pour broth and an equal amount of water into a saucepan. Bring to boil over medium heat. Add rice and cook 10 minutes. Drain in colander (spaghetti strainer) and serve.

Comments:

Another "no-brainer" side dish. The flavor of the broth adds little fat to the dish. The nutrition information has been adjusted to reflect this.

Nutritional Information:

	Rice	Broth
Fat 2.2 g	1.2	1.0
Calories	111	15
Fat Percent	10%	60%

Serve with:

Salmon with Appeal (p. 6)

Foiled Again Fillets (p. 5)

Sea Bass á Teriyaki (p. 19)

Grilled Eggplant Chips

Ingredients:

1 Italian Eggplant (1/4 lb)

1 teaspoon Garlic Salt

1 teaspoon Olive Oil (optional)

1 teaspoon Soy Sauce (optional)

Instructions:

Preheat the broiler. Cut the eggplant into about 1/4" slices (about 10 of them) and discard both ends of the eggplant. Lay them out on a piece of aluminum foil in a single layer. Sprinkle with the garlic salt (or optionally brush with oil and then sprinkle) and broil 2 minutes per side about 4 inches from the broiler elements. (Watch the eggplant chips carefully and flip after two minutes or as soon as the centers start to brown. Don't allow to cook more or they will burn.)

Comments:

The small Italian eggplant makes a perfect side dish for one, especially if you are already broiling. Without the oil this is a no fat, delicious and real "no-brainer" recipe!

Nutritional Information:

	Eggplant
Fat 0 g	0
Calories	13
Fat Percent	0%

Serve with:

Foiled Again Fillets (p. 5)

Lamb Chops with Shallot (p. 7)

Sea Bass á Teriyaki (p. 19)

▼

Grilled Tomato Slices

Ingredients:

1 large Tomato

2 teaspoons Oregano

1 teaspoon Olive Oil (optional)

Instructions:

Slice the tomato into thick 1/2 inch slices. (A large tomato should yield about 3 or 4 slices.) Discard ends. Place slices in a single layer on a piece of aluminum foil. Top with oregano. If broiling, set in oven about 4 inches from elements. If grilling, place on grill and pierce foil to allow tomatoes to grill. Cook 6 minutes.

Comments:

As an option, you can top each slice with an equal amount of the olive oil.

Nutritional Information:

	Tomato
Fat .3 g	.3
Calories	24
Fat Percent	11%

Serve with:

Lamb Chops with Shallot (p. 7)

Coney Island Chili (p. 11)

Mussels in Wine (p. 76)

▼

Lemon & Pepper Angel Pasta

Ingredients:

1 cup Angel Hair Pasta (about 1 oz.)

2 teaspoons Lemon Juice

**1/8 tablespoon Pepper
(one twist of a pepper mill)**

1/2 teaspoon Parsley

Instructions:

Cook pasta in boiling water for 2 minutes. Drain into a colander (spaghetti strainer) and rinse in hot water. Prevents sticking together due to loose flour on the pasta. Add lemon juice, pepper and parsley and toss well. Serve on warm plate.

Comments:

This is a nearly no fat side dish that cooks up in two minutes. Angel hair pasta sticks together quite a bit if not cooked in a lot of water. Also, be sure to serve on a hot plate or the pasta will get cold very quickly.

Nutritional Information:

	Pasta
Fat	1 g	1
Calories	159
Fat Percent	6%

Serve with:

Teriyaki Chicken (p. 13)

Veal Mushrooms and Wine (p. 22)

Steak Diane (p. 23)

Appetizers • Starters

▼

Tomato Mozzarella Salad

Ingredients:

1 medium Tomato

4 oz. Mozzarella Cheese

1/4 cup Basil Leaves, fresh

**1/4 cup Italian Dressing
(e.g. Paul Newman's)**

Instructions:

Slice tomato into 12 pieces. (Cut the tomato in half, slice each half into thirds, and then half again.) Cube mozzarella into 16 pieces. (4 oz. is half of a standard 8 oz. block of mozzarella.) Snip basil Leaves into small pieces using scissors. Place all ingredients into a bowl and toss until dressing coats everything and tomato, basil and cheese are attractively mixed.

Comments:

As an alternate presentation, slice the cheese and tomatoes into 4 to 6 round slices. Lay the cheese, tomato, and whole basil leaves alternately and slightly overlapping on a small serving plate and cover with 1/4 cup of dressing.

Nutritional Information:

	Mozzarella	Dressing
Fat 56 g	24	32
Calories	320	300
Fat Percent	68%	96%

Serve with:

Veal Piccata (p. 4)

Roast Garlic Chicken (p. 14)

Veal Mushrooms and Wine (p. 22)

French Onion Soup

Ingredients:

1 cup Onion (finely sliced)

1 tablespoon Butter

1 cup Beef Broth*

1 slice Provolone Cheese

1 1/2" slice from French Roll

Instructions:

Turn oven on broil. In a small frying pan sauté sliced onions in the butter on stove over medium heat until they are translucent, but not yet browned (about 6 minutes). Meanwhile, heat broth in a sauce pan over low heat. Add finished onions and any sauce to the broth and heat for an additional minute. Ladle soup into an oven proof bowl. Top with the slice of bread and then cheese and broil until the cheese melts (about 1 1/2 minutes).

Comments:

One medium onion will make about one cup sliced.

*Canned broth (double strength) is fine to use; however, mix the broth with about 3/4 cup of water before measuring out 1 cup. If you like the broth stronger or weaker, add more broth or water after tasting.

Nutritional Information:

	Onion	Butter	Broth	Cheese	Bread
Fat 21 g	.4	12.3	.5	7.6	.2
Calories	54	111	33	100	69
Fat Percent	7%	100%	14%	68%	3%

Serve with

Garlic Chicken Puffs (p. 10)

Pesto Pasta (p. 12)

Steak Diane (p. 23)

▼

Mandarin Spinach Salad

Ingredients:

6 large Spinach Leaves, fresh

5 Mandarin Orange Slices

2 tablespoons chopped Hard Boiled Egg

2 tablespoons Vinaigrette Salad Dressing

Instructions:

Arrange leaves on small salad plate. Sprinkle with egg and arrange orange slices over leaves. Top with salad dressing. It's best to use only the egg whites to save on fat and cholesterol.
(White= 0 g fat and 16 calories vs. Yolk= 5.6 g fat and 63 calories)

Comments:

This simple combination of flavors is excellent. All the ingredients can be obtained from the salad bar. Make sure to keep items separate (especially the spinach) before serving so they will be crisp when dinner is ready. (Use separate containers if necessary.)

Nutritional Information:

	Egg	Dressing
Fat	7.5 g	0	7.5
Calories	16	69
Fat Percent	0%	98%

Serve with:

Lemon Chicken (p. 2)

Roast Garlic Chicken (p. 14)

Orange Roughy (p. 17)

Hot Brie Dip

Ingredients:

4 oz. round of Brie cheese

1 Hard Roll (slightly larger than Brie)

Instructions:

Preheat oven to 375°. Use Brie to trace and cut a circle in the top of roll the same size as the Brie. Remove the cut bread within the traced area of the roll to form a small "bowl" that the Brie will fit into nicely. Insert Brie and bake for 15 minutes. Peel top white layer of Brie and stir melted cheese. If the cheese isn't all melted, return to oven for 2 minutes. Serve.

Comments:

The roll hardens as it bakes to form a hard bowl. This is nice as a before dinner appetizer for two. The fat content for one person is in the "don't ask, don't tell" range. (This could take all your fat grams for one day.) To make a serving for parties, use larger Brie and a large sourdough loaf.

Nutritional Information:

	Brie	Bread
Fat 31.9 g	31.5	.4
Calories	360	137
Fat Percent	79%	3%

Serve with

Pasta Quick (p. 3)

Veal Piccata (p. 4)

Scallops Toronado (p. 27)

▼

Asparagus Vinaigrette

Ingredients:

1 15 oz. can Asparagus Spears

**1/4 cup Italian Dressing
(e.g. Paul Newman's)**

Instructions:

Open and drain asparagus spears. Add Italian dressing and allow to marinate about 10 minutes before serving. Transfer to serving plate.

Comments:

When you open the top of a can of asparagus spears, you find the bottom of the spears. This allows you to pour out the asparagus without breaking the tips. For this recipe, it also makes it easy to marinate the tips.

Nutritional Information:

	Dressing
Fat 16 g	16
Calories	146
Fat Percent	99%

Serve with:

Salmon with Appeal (p. 6)

Fettuccine Alfredo (p. 18)

Spaghetti with Mussels (p. 25)

Spinach Things

Ingredients:

1 tablespoon Butter

1 clove Shallot (minced)

1 cup fresh Spinach (14 large leaves)

2 tablespoons Feta Cheese

4 pieces Crescent Roll dough

Instructions:

Preheat oven to 350°. In a saucepan, heat butter and well-minced shallot. After 2 minutes, add spinach and cook until spinach is wilted (3 minutes). Add feta cheese and stir for 30 seconds. Place crescent dough on a cookie sheet and top each with a quarter of the mixture. Seal dough loosely and bake 10 minutes at 350°.

Comments:

Crescent roll dough is found in the refrigerated section of the grocery store. Spinach things make great appetizers for parties. Make twice as many by splitting the crescent roll dough into eight triangles and distributing the mixture over the eight pastries.

Nutritional Information:

	Crescent	Butter	Feta
Fat 23.4 g	5	12.4	6
Calories	100	112	75
Fat Percent	45%	100%	72%

Serve with:

Pesto Pasta (p. 12)

Roast Garlic Chicken (p. 14)

Steak Diane (p. 23)

Quesedillas

Ingredients:

1 Flour Tortilla

2 tablespoons Cheddar Cheese (grated)

2 tablespoons Scallions (chopped)

Instructions:

Place flour tortilla on medium hot griddle or in large frying pan. Top with grated cheese and chopped scallions. Heat about 1 minute until cheese is melted. Fold tortilla in half over cheese and remove from pan. Slice tortilla crosswise into finger-size slices.

Comments:

This makes nice soft tortilla appetizers. For a crisper tortilla, use the same recipe but broil in the oven on a cookie sheet instead of pan frying.

Nutritional Information:

	Tortilla	Cheese
Fat 7.4 g	2.5	4.9
Calories	110	57
Fat Percent	20%	77%

Serve with:

Fajita (p. 9)

Teriyaki Chicken (p. 13)

Grilled Pizza (p. 31)

Pot Stickers

Ingredients:

1/4 lb. Ground Pork

2 teaspoons Soy Sauce

1/2 teaspoon Scallions (white part only)

8 Wonton Wrappers

1 tablespoon Oil (optional)

Instructions:

Mix together the ground pork, soy sauce and scallions. Place one teaspoon in the center of each of 8 wonton wrappers. Brush the edges of the wrappers with water and fold the wrapper over the pork filling to form a small triangle. Press the open edges to seal. (Some meat will be left over.) Now place the pot stickers in a steamer and steam for 3 minutes until cooked. Alternately, they may also be fried in 1 tablespoon of oil in a saucepan. Fry about 2 minutes (until brown, flip over and fry 2 more minutes.)

Comments:

Make a quick dipping sauce for the pot stickers using 2 tablespoons of soy sauce, and mixing in the white part of one scallion.

Nutritional Information:

	Pork	Wonton
Fat 9.6 g	9.6	0
Calories	219	60
Fat Percent	39%	0%

Serve with:

Lemon Chicken (p. 2)

Teriyaki Chicken (p. 13)

Fried Rice (p. 32)

Caviar Potatoes

Ingredients:

4 New Potatoes*

4 teaspoons Sour Cream

**1 teaspoon Caviar
(Whitefish or Lumpfish)**

Instructions:

Boil potatoes in water for 18 minutes. Drain potatoes. Carefully, scoop a small well into one side of a potato using a small spoon or a melon baller. Fill the well with 1 teaspoon of sour cream. Top sour cream with small amount of caviar. Repeat for other three potatoes.

Comments:

These can be served or cold. Both are equally delicious. If you are having guests and want to go the extra step, you can pipe the sour cream into the potato with a pastry bag using a decorative tip.

*These are the small potatoes about "2 diameter which are also known as creamer potatoes.

Nutritional Information:

	Potato	Sour Cream
Fat 5.2 g	.2	5
Calories	220	60
Fat Percent	1%	75%

Serve with:

Lamb Chops with Shallot (p. 7)

Teriyaki Chicken (p. 13)

Steak Diane (p. 23)

Shrimp Cocktail

Ingredients:

5 medium cooked Shrimp

1/2 cup Lettuce Leaves (any kind)

1/4 Lemon

2 tablespoons Ketchup

1 teaspoon Horseradish

Instructions:

Fill the bottom of a red wine glass (wide type glass) with shredded lettuce leaves. Mix ketchup and horseradish (this makes cocktail sauce) and spoon onto lettuce. Make a small cut across the underside of each shrimp. Arrange the five shrimp on the lip of the wine glass. The cut will hold the shrimp in place. Add the lemon in the same manner.

Comments:

Arrange shrimp at the 10, 11, 12, 1 and 2 o'clock positions around the glass. Place the lemon at the 6 o'clock position.

Nutritional Information:

	Shrimp	Lemon
Fat 1.81 g	1.8	.01
Calories	91	9
Fat Percent	18%	1%

Serve with:

Lamb Chops with Shallot (p. 7)

Veal Mushrooms and Wine (p. 22)

Steak Diane (p. 23)

Garlic Shrimp Grill Skewers

Ingredients:

4 medium Shrimp (raw)

2 tablespoons Butter

2 Cloves Garlic (crushed)

1/2 teaspoon Parsley

Instructions:

Peel and butterfly the shrimp. (To butterfly shrimp: Break off the shell and peel it off. Then use a sharp knife to cut along the entire back curve of the shrimp about 1/4" deep.) Thread the four shrimp on a wooden or metal skewer. Melt butter in microwave or stove and mix in the garlic and parsley. Brush all sides of the shrimp with mixture. Grill on barbecue (or 4" under broiler) for 3 minutes. Turn skewer over and brush again with butter, and cook an additional 2 minutes.

Comments:

When cooking the shrimp using this method, not much of the 2 tablespoons of butter stays on the shrimp. The nutrition information has been adjusted to reflect this.

Nutritional Information:

	Shrimp	Butter
Fat 5.9 g	1.8	4.1
Calories	91	37
Fat Percent	18%	100%

Serve with:

Pesto Pasta (p. 12)

Beef in Wok (p. 16)

Steak Diane (p. 23)

▼

California Rolls

Ingredients:

1/2 cup Rice

1 sheet Nori

1/2 Avocado

1 oz. Imitation Crab

Instructions:

"Quick cook" rice 10 minutes and drain. Place nori on a sheet of wax paper. Cool rice and spread evenly over nori. Place thin slices of avocado and crab on one edge of nori. Starting at the filling, roll the package jelly-roll style using the wax paper as an aid. (Don't roll in the wax paper.) Slice roll into 6 even pieces.

Comments:

For advanced students, flip the whole package onto another piece of wax paper and roll with the rice side out. Press 1 tablespoon sesame seeds into sides. Also serve with soy sauce for dipping (and wasabi).

The trick to sushi dishes is sticky rice. This is best done by using short grain rice and cooking it quickly. Spread cooked rice on a cookie sheet and cool it by fanning it.

Nutritional Information:

	Rice	Avocado	Crab
Fat 16.76 g	1.2	15	.56
Calories	111	153	38
Fat Percent	10%	88%	13%

Serve with:

Salmon with Appeal (p. 6)

Teriyaki Chicken (p. 13)

Fried Rice (p. 32)

▼

Grilled Lemon Scallops

Ingredients:

13 small Scallops

2 tablespoons (1/4 stick) Butter

2 tablespoons White Wine

1 tablespoon Lemon Juice

Instructions:

Melt the butter and combine in a small bowl with wine and lemon juice. Toss all the scallops in the butter mixture until well coated. Place scallops on grill or broiler pan and broil about three minutes, turning occasionally, until scallops are opaque and start to shrink. Brush once a minute with butter mixture.

Comments:

Since the butter mixture is used as a marinade, all of the 2 tablespoons is not contained in the final dish. The nutritional information has been adjusted to reflect this. Also, when grilling, the scallops will shrink just as they are finished cooking and before they are overcooked and dry. You may want to place one scallop on the grill 30 seconds ahead of the others as the indicator of when the scallops are ready.

Nutritional Information:

	Scallops	Butter
Fat 5.3 g	1.2	4.1
Calories	81	37
Fat Percent	13%	100%

Serve with:

Pasta Quick (p. 3)

Pesto Pasta (p. 12)

Fried Rice (p. 32)

Feta Tomato Salad

Ingredients:

4 Cherry Tomatoes

1 tablespoon Feta Cheese

1 clove Shallot (minced well)

**1 tablespoon Italian Dressing
(Paul Newman's is best)**

Instructions:

Cut the tomatoes into quarters, removing the small stem on top. In a small bowl, add tomatoes, crumble the feta cheese, and add the finely cut-up Shallot. Toss. Add the dressing and toss gently again.

Comments:

After arranging this salad on the serving plate, you may want to top it with a small sprinkle of oregano, for an even better flavor.

Nutritional Information:

Fat 14.3 g	Tomato	Cheese	Dressing
Fat 14.3 g	.3	6	8
Calories	24	75	75
Fat Percent	11%	72%	96%

Serve with:

Fajita (p. 9)
Roast Garlic Chicken (p. 14)
Steak Diane (p. 23)

▼

Good Salad

Ingredients:

1 cup Lettuce (Romaine is best)

4 Green Onions (scallions)

1 tablespoon Dill

2 tablespoons Vegetable Oil

1 tablespoon Red Vinegar

Instructions:

Bunch up the lettuce and slice into 1/4" strips. Toss into large bowl for mixing. Slice green onion into thin slices (use only the white part; the rest is not eaten) and add to bowl. Snip 1 tablespoon of dill into bowl using scissors. Toss all ingredients. In a blender or cup, blend the oil and vinegar well. Pour over salad and toss. Serve.

Comments:

The lettuce and other ingredients can once again be taken from the salad bar. About 1 cup makes a large salad for one, or two smaller salads for two.

Nutritional Information:

	Oil
Fat 28 g	28
Calories	253
Fat Percent	100%

Serve with:

Lemon Chicken (p. 2)

Lamb Chops with Shallot (p. 7)

Steak Diane (p. 23)

Stuffed Mushrooms

Ingredients:

4 large Mushrooms

1 tablespoon Butter

1 tablespoon Onion (minced)

2 tablespoons Bread Crumbs

1/2 cup Beef Broth (or beef bouillon cube in 1/2 cup water)

Instructions:

Preheat oven to 500°. Remove stems from mushrooms and mince. In small saucepan over medium heat, sauté mushrooms with onion and butter for 3 minutes. Add bread crumbs and remove from heat. Stuff 1/4 of the mixture into each of the mushroom caps. Place them cup side up in a small, oven-proof dish, add broth to dish and bake at 500° for 10 minutes.

Comments:

To prevent waste, purchase onion from the salad bar. Also, 1 slice of toasted bread will yield about 4 tablespoons of bread crumbs. If you use an all-metal skillet, it can go right from the stove top to the oven, saving you from washing one more dish.

Nutritional Information:

	Mushroom	Butter	Bread
Fat 12.9g	.2	12.3	.4
Calories	9	111	42
Fat Percent	20%	100%	9%

Serve with:

Lamb Chops with Shallot (p. 7)

Teriyaki Chicken (p. 13)

Veal Mushrooms and Wine (p. 22)

Mussels in Wine

Ingredients:

12 Mussels

5 cloves Garlic (crushed)

1/2 cup White Wine

Instructions:

Rinse mussels under cold water and pull off any stringy attachments. Good mussels should be clean and the shells closed. Add all ingredients to small, covered saucepan. Mussels will not be fully submerged, and don't have to be, because they will cook by "steaming". Bring pan to a boil. Reduce heat to low, and cook for four minutes. Dump entire contents of pot into serving bowl. Discard any mussels that haven't opened. (These are not edible.)

Comments:

The liquid acts as flavoring for the mussels and as a dip when eating them. You can add 1 tablespoon of butter or additional spices to the liquid during or after steaming mussels to add more flavor.

Nutritional Information:

	Mussels
Fat 2.2 g	2.2
Calories	95
Fat Percent	21%

Serve with:

Pasta Quick (p. 3)

Pesto Pasta (p. 12)

Fettuccine Alfredo (p. 18)

Asparagus with Faux Bernaise

Ingredients:

1/4 cup Shallot (minced)

3 tablespoons White Wine

1/2 teaspoon Tarragon

2 tablespoons Sour Cream

6 fresh Asparagus Stalks

Instructions:

Cover asparagus with water in a medium sauce pan and boil three minutes. Drain and set on serving plate. In a medium saucepan, cook shallots, wine and tarragon until it boils. Continue boiling for 1 minute. Pour into strainer to separate solids and liquids. Discard the solids and add sour cream to the liquid. Mix and pour over asparagus.

Comments:

Bernaise sauce is generally made the same way, but butter is used instead of sour cream. This version is much lower in fat and made faster.

Nutritional Information:

	Cream	Asparagus
Fat 6.2 g	5.9	.3
Calories	62	22
Fat Percent	86%	12%

Serve with:

Lemon Chicken (p. 2)

Veal Piccata (p. 4)

Steak Diane (p. 23)

▼

Japanese Spinach Salad

Ingredients:

8 large Spinach Leaves, fresh (2 oz.)

1 tablespoon Soy Sauce

1/2 teaspoon Sherry

2/3 teaspoon Sugar

Instructions:

Break off the stems from the spinach leaves and wash the leaves. Do not shake off the water. Place them in a covered, medium saucepan over medium heat for 6 minutes (or till they wilt.) Drain excess water and place leaves on serving plate. Mix remaining ingredients in a small bowl and spoon about 2 teaspoons of this dressing over leaves.

Comments:

If you wish, you can toast about 1 tablespoon of sesame seeds, and add them to the salad. This adds a nice flavor.

Nutritional Information:

	Spinach	Sugar
Fat	.4 g .4	0
Calories	42	31
Fat Percent	9%	0%

Serve with:

Beef in Wok (p. 16)

Tuna Steak (p. 20)

Fried Rice (p. 32)

▼

Blair Pea Soup

Ingredients:

2 tablespoons Onion, minced (1/2 small Onion)

1/2 teaspoon Olive Oil

1/4 cup Chicken Stock

1/4 cup Peas

1/4 cup Milk

Instructions:

In a small skillet, sauté onions in olive oil over medium heat 5 minutes or until browned. Add chicken stock and peas, and cook 2 minutes. Pour mixture into blender and puree 30 seconds. Add milk and mix a few seconds more. Return to skillet for 2 minutes, warming until heated through.

Comments:

Peas are practically the perfect vegetable. They are higher in fiber than any other common vegetable, have virtually no fat and are available ready to eat. Have them as a side dish as often as possible; but when you have ten extra minutes preparation time, this soup is a great change of pace!

Nutritional Information:

	Oil	Stock	Milk	Peas
Fat 14 g	2.1	.2	2	.1
Calories	19	9	37	33
Fat Percent	100%	20%	49%	3%

Serve with:

Lemon Chicken (p. 2)

Veal Picatta (p. 4)

Fettuccine Alfredo (p. 18)

Ebi

Ingredients:

2 large Shrimp

1/4 cup medium-grain Rice, uncooked

3/4 cup Water

1/4 teaspoon Horseradish (or Wasabe, Japanese Horseradish)

Instructions:

If shrimp is not already cooked, boil in a large pot of water for 3 minutes. Cool and peel. Boil 3/4 cup of water and add rice. Stir after 1 minute and every 3 minutes after that for 10 minutes. Remove and spread rice on waxed paper to cool. When cool, form into two mounds. Split back of shrimp and flatten them on counter. Spread half of horseradish on bottom of each shrimp. Place one on each rice mound, and place on plate.

Comments:

Ebi, a common sushi offering, is simply a butterflied shrimp with a bit of horseradish on a small mound of rice. The key is making the rice very sticky, which happens when the rice cools. Use the waxed paper to form the mounds so the rice doesn't stick to your hands.

Nutritional Information:

	Shrimp	Rice
Fat 2.4 g	1.8	.6
Calories	91	56
Fat Percent	18%	10%

Serve with:

Teriaki Chicken (p. 13)

Beef in Wok (p. 16)

Scallops Toronado (p. 27)

▼

Beer Boiled Shrimp

Ingredients:

3/4 cup Beer

2 teaspoons Parsley, chopped

1/2 teaspoon Tabasco Sauce

1 tablespoon Lemon Juice (1/2 a lemon)

1/2 lb. Shrimp, raw or cooked (about 10 small)

Instructions:

Boil the beer, parsley, tabasco, and lemon in a small skillet over medium heat. When the mixture has reached a full boil, add peeled shrimp. Cook for 3 minutes if using raw or frozen shrimp, and 1 1/2 minutes if using thawed pre-cooked shrimp. The liquid should fully cover the shrimp. The shrimp will be white when cooked. After cooking, scoop shrimp onto a serving plate and top with 1 tablespoon of the beer mixture.

Comments:

When serving this as an appetizer you can melt 2 tablespoons of butter to use for dipping the shrimp. This will add 5 grams of fat to the meal.

Nutritional Information:

	Beer	Shrimp
Fat 1.8 g	0	1.8
Calories	40	91
Fat Percent	0%	18%

Serve with:

Veal Picatta (p. 4)

Beef in Wok (p. 16)

Steak Diane (p. 23)

▼

Bread Pudding

Ingredients:

1 stale Dinner Roll
(about hamburger roll size)

1/2 cup Egg Nog

2 tablespoons Sugar

2 tablespoons Raisins

Instructions:

Preheat oven to 450°. Break up the roll into small pieces no bigger than about 1/2" thick. Start adding egg nog a little at a time and stir until the mixture is the consistency of oatmeal and all the bread is moist. Do not add more egg nog than needed. Mix in the Sugar and raisins. Pour mixture into 8" cake pan (it will form one small layer). Cook about 18 minutes or until the top starts to brown. Remove carefully and slice into wedges. Serve.

Comments:

This is a novelty recipe that's great to try around Christmas time. The recipe really does require stale bread. It just won't work with fresh bread. In the unlikely event that you don't have a dried roll, toast the bread first to dry it out. Most types of bread will work for this recipe.

This is nice as a dessert as well. Try it in with a little Bourbon over it like they do in New Orleans.

Nutritional Information:

	Roll	Egg Nog
Fat 9.4 g	.4	9
Calories	137	171
Fat Percent	3%	47%

Serve with:

Fajita (p. 9)
Coney Island Chili (p. 11)
Spaghetti with Mussels (p. 25)

Desserts

Chocolate Soufflé

Ingredients:

1 oz. Semi-Sweet Chocolate (melted & cooled)

1 Egg White

Instructions:

Preheat oven to 375°. Beat egg white to stiff peaks. Fold in melted chocolate carefully. Pour mixture into 1-1/4 cup soufflé dish or mug. Bake 10 minutes until well risen.

Comments:

To prevent sticking, grease cup with butter and powder with confectioner's sugar. Variations: Add 1 tablespoon Amaretto liqueur, just before folding in chocolate. Top with confectioner's sugar for appearance.

Nutritional Information:

	Egg	Chocolate
Fat 7.8 g	0	7.8
Calories	16	140
Fat Percent	0%	50%

Serve with:

Lemon Chicken (p. 2)

Veal Piccata (p. 4)

Steak Diane (p. 23)

▼

Bananas Foster

Ingredients:

2 Bananas (cut in half lengthwise)

2 tablespoons Butter

2 tablespoons Brown Sugar

2 teaspoons Lemon

3 tablespoons Rum (at room temperature)

Instructions:

Melt butter in a skillet. Sauté bananas, sugar and lemon until softened and brown. Add rum to pan and "flambé". Stir until flames die.

Comments:

Added touches: One scoop good quality vanilla ice cream and 1 teaspoon shavings from orange peel. This is the dessert that supposedly burned down Brennen's of New Orleans' first restaurant.

Nutritional Information:

	Butter	Sugar	Banana
Fat 25.2 g	24	0	1.2
Calories	216	92	210
Fat Percent	100%	0%	5%

Serve with:

Lemon Chicken (p. 2)

Pasta Quick (p. 3)

Veal Mushrooms and Wine (p. 22)

Amaretto Strawberries

Ingredients:

2 cups Strawberries

1/4 cup Raspberry Jam

2 tablespoons Amaretto

Instructions:

Cut strawberries into halves or quarters. Toss with jam and Amaretto. Serve in a martini glass. Top with dab of sour cream or fresh whipped cream and mint leaf if desired.

Comments:

Using the all-fruit type jams gives this the best flavor. Microwave the jam slightly (approximately 15 seconds) to soften it and allow it to mix easily. This recipe can be prepared ahead of dinner and kept refrigerated until ready to serve!

Nutritional Information:

	Strawberries	Jam
Fat 0.4 g	0.4	0
Calories	90	108
Fat Percent	4%	0%

Serve with:

Salmon with Appeal (p. 6)

Fettuccine Alfredo (p. 18)

Breaded Veal (p. 30)

Le Colonel

Ingredients:

1 scoop Lemon Sherbet

1 tablespoon Vodka (good quality)

Instructions:

Place vodka in a nice long stem wine or dessert glass. Top with scoop of sherbet.

Comments:

This is the traditional dish found in all Swiss restaurants. It is unclear where the name comes from. The sherbet and vodka mix settles heavy meals nicely.

Nutritional Information:

	Sherbet
Fat 1.5 g	1.5
Calories	110
Fat Percent	12%

Serve with:

Salmon with Appeal (p. 6)

Pesto Pasta (p. 12)

Fettuccine Alfredo (p. 18)

Raspberry Sauce

Ingredients:

1 pint Raspberries (fresh or frozen)

1 teaspoon Vanilla Extract

2 Pear Halves (canned)

Instructions:

Blend raspberries in blender and pour into strainer. Push blended berries through strainer to remove seeds and catch sauce in a small bowl. Add vanilla to sauce and stir. Place two pear halves face down on a dessert plate and pour the sauce carefully around the pears. (Use only as much as needed.) Add mint leaves for decor.

Comments:

The basic sauce has lots of uses. Try it around a piece of store-bought cheese cake or over fruit. This is a very attractive and classic presentation for dessert.

Nutritional Information:

	Raspberry	Pear
Fat	0.3 g	0.2	0.1
Calories	61	50
Fat Percent	3%	2%

Serve with:

Lemon Chicken (p. 2)

Salmon with Appeal (p. 6)

Orange Roughy (p. 17)

▼

Crêpes

Ingredients:

1/4 cup Skim Milk

1 Egg White

2 tablespoons Flour

3 tablespoons Strawberry All-Fruit Jam

Instructions:

Blend the milk, egg and flour together. Mix well. Put a little oil or butter in 8" frying pan and heat. When oil smokes a little, wipe pan clean with paper towel, add 2 tablespoons of batter and spread thin by tilting pan. After 30 seconds the crêpe will look dry and the edges will curl up. Slip spatula under crêpe and flip. Cook 30 seconds more and slide out of pan onto a plate. Add fruit filling and fold in quarters. Makes 3 crêpes.

Comments:

The crêpe should be just slightly brown when cooked. Adjust the heat up or down if the first one is too pale or too dark. Chocolate shavings, sour cream and a variety of jams all make great fillers for the crêpes.

Nutritional Information:

	Milk	Egg White	Flour
Fat .25 g	.10	0.1	.05
Calories	21	16	54
Fat Percent	4%	0%	3%

Serve with:

Lemon Chicken (p. 2)

Pasta Quick (p. 3)

Shrimp Scampi (p. 28)

▼

Grand Marnier Oranges

Ingredients:

1 large Orange

4 teaspoons Grand Marnier

Instructions:

Slice the orange crossways to get five nice 1/4" slices about the same size. Remove the rind carefully with a sharp knife. Place the five slices in a circle on a small salad plate so they all touch in the center of the plate and overlap each other. Drizzle the Grand Marnier over the orange slices.

Comments:

The key to this dessert (as simple as it is) is to serve it at room temperature. If cold, the flavors will be masked.

Nutritional Information:

	Orange
Fat .2 g	.2
Calories	65
Fat Percent	3%

Serve with:

Pasta Quick (p. 3)

Veal Piccata (p. 4)

Fettuccine Alfredo (p. 18)

▼

Chocolate Fondue

Ingredients:

1/4 cup Semi-Sweet Chocolate Drops (3 oz.)

2 tablespoons Cream (liquid, not whipped)

1 teaspoon Grand Marnier (optional)

1 Pear (cut roughly into 1" pieces)

Instructions:

Over very low heat, melt the chocolate. After about 3 minutes the semi-sweet drops will appear shiny. At this point they are melted. Stir with a dry spoon to check. Add cream and liquor and stir until smooth. Reduce heat to warm. Fondue is ready. Bring it to the table. Use a fork to dip the pear pieces into the chocolate and enjoy.

Comments:

Different fruits are also good with this dish, such as bananas, white grapes or apples. As a point of protocol: in France, where this dish was developed, it is considered poor manners to eat the entire dish while standing over the stove!

Nutritional Information:

	Chocolate	Cream
Fat 56 g	45	12
Calories	429	108
Fat Percent	94%	100%

Serve with:

Lemon Chicken (p. 2)

Pasta Quick (p. 3)

Roast Garlic Chicken (p. 14)

Kahlúa Vanilla Nuts

Ingredients:

1 scoop Vanilla Ice Cream (good quality)

1 tablespoon Kahlúa

2 teaspoons Walnuts

Instructions:

Place ice cream in a martini glass and surround with Kahlúa. Break walnuts into small pieces over ice cream.

Comments:

This dessert is high in fat, mostly because of the nuts. This demonstrates again how easy it can be to cut the fat in your diet with small changes.
49 grams of fat could be your limit for the day and be consumed by this dessert. Leave off the nuts and it's only 11 grams of fat.

Nutritional Information:

	Ice Cream	Walnuts
Fat 49 g	11	38
Calories	175	380
Fat Percent	57%	90%

Serve with:

Pasta Quick (p. 3)

Pesto Pasta (p. 12)

Veal Mushrooms and Wine (p. 22)

Oslo Ice Cream

Ingredients:

**1 scoop Vanilla Ice Cream
(good quality)**

1 tablespoon Bailey's Irish Creme

**Chocolate Shavings
(from a chocolate bar)**

Instructions:

Place ice cream in martini glass and cover with Bailey's Irish cream liqueur. Sprinkle with shavings carved from a chocolate bar using a potato peeler or cheese grater.

Comments:

This is a nice dessert after a meal and seems to be a favorite in Norwegian restaurants.

Nutritional Information:

	Ice Cream	Bailey's
Fat	4.1 g	3.1	1
Calories	91	20
Fat Percent	31%	45%

Serve with:

Pasta Quick (p. 3)

Pesto Pasta (p. 12)

Veal Mushrooms and Wine (p. 22)

▼

Blueberries and Cream

Ingredients:

1/2 cup Blueberries (50 of them)

2 tablespoons heavy Cream (liquid not whipped)

1/4 teaspoon Sugar

Instructions:

Combine the cream and sugar until the sugar dissolves. Add mixture to the bottom of a martini glass. Add blueberries. As an addition, you can add 1/4 teaspoon of bourbon whiskey to the cream.

Comments:

This is a tasty dessert, but the blueberries can be very expensive off-season, especially if you don't live in Florida or California.

Nutritional Information:

	Cream	Sugar
Fat 12 g	12	0
Calories	108	12
Fat Percent	100%	0%

Serve with:

Veal Piccata (p. 4)

Veal Mushrooms and Wine (p. 22)

Steak Diane (p. 23)

Peanut Butter Cookie Quickie

Ingredients:

2 tablespoons Peanut Butter

2 tablespoons Sugar

1 1/2 teaspoons Egg (beaten)

Instructions:

Preheat oven to 350°. Beat the 1 1/2 teaspoons of egg in a cup slightly and add to a small bowl with sugar and peanut butter. Mix well and divide into four pieces. Drop pieces onto a cake pan or cookie sheet and cook for 13 minutes or until cookies are brown on the edges and top.

Comments:

An egg is generally about 1/4 cup of liquid. This recipe calls for 1 1/2 teaspoons of egg and the rest can be discarded.

Nutritional Information:

	Peanut Butter	Sugar	Egg
Fat 16.7 g	16	0	.7
Calories	188	92	9
Fat Percent	77%	0%	70%

Serve with:

Lemon Chicken (p. 2)

Coney Island Chili (p. 11)

Little Foot Pizza (p. 15)

Chocolate Cream Pie

Ingredients:

5 Oreo Cookies (crushed well)

1 tablespoon Butter (melted)

1/2 cup Whipped Cream (non-dairy)

1 oz. Semi-Sweet Chocolate (melted)

Instructions:

Blend the cookie crumbs and butter well. Press the mixture onto the inside and bottom of a small Pyrex™ or similar bowl that is about 3" wide and 2" deep. (You could even use a shallow coffee cup.) Mix the cream and chocolate until well blended and spoon into bowl. Freeze dessert for about 10 minutes. (Longer is OK.)

Comments:

If you are brave, turn dessert over when ready and rap on counter to knock it out of bowl. Place it back, face up on a serving plate. This is a great quick dessert if you pick up the cookies from the bulk food bins. (Buying a whole bag of cookies to obtain the ten needed for this recipe may tend to increase your fat intake for the day.)

Nutritional Information:

	Cookies	Butter	Cream	Chocolate
Fat 34.7 g	11.6	12.3	3	7.8
Calories	267	111	50	140
Fat Percent	39%	100%	54%	50%

Serve with:

Garlic Chicken Puffs (p. 10)

Steak Diane (p. 23)

Grilled Pizza (p. 31)

Apple Compote

Ingredients:

1 small Apple (Staymans are best)

1 tablespoon Butter

1 tablespoon Brown Sugar

1 tablespoon Raisins

Instructions:

Peel and slice the apple into eight segments. Place in a small microwaveable bowl. Cut up the butter into small pieces and distribute all over the apples. Sprinkle with the sugar. Microwave for four minutes. Remove from oven, add the raisins and toss mixture.

Comments:

This is a quick microwave dessert. If you can spare the fat calories, a scoop of good quality vanilla ice cream is a great addition to this recipe.

Nutritional Information:

	Apple	Butter	Sugar	Raisins
Fat 12.8 g	.4	12.3	0	.1
Calories	81	111	46	56
Fat Percent	4%	100%	0%	2%

Serve with:

Lamb Chops with Shallot (p. 7)

Roast Garlic Chicken (p. 14)

Steak Diane (p. 23)

Baked Alaska

Ingredients:

1 large Cookie (3" wide)

**1 scoop Vanilla Ice Cream
(or 3 oz. Ice Cream Cup)**

1 Egg White

1 tablespoon Sugar

Instructions:

Preheat oven to 450°. Place the cookie on a cookie sheet covered with aluminum foil. Top the cookie with the ice cream. The cookie should be large enough so that there is about 1/2" between the ice cream and the edge of the cookie all around. In a bowl, beat egg white and slowly add sugar until all egg white is stiff. Spread egg white over ice cream assuring that it is completely covered with egg white. Bake 5 minutes or until dessert is brown. Serve.

Comments:

It is important that the egg white topping completely cover the Ice cream. This means the cookie should be big enough. (Get a big one from the bakery of your grocery store.) Watch especially that the egg white seals well to the edge of the cookie, or the ice cream will melt and leak out. Also, a slice of pound cake can be used instead of the cookie as long as it is large enough.

Nutritional Information:

	Cookie	Ice Cream	Egg White	Sugar
Fat 10.2 g	3	7.2	0	0
Calories	83	134	16	46
Fat Percent	33%	48%	0%	0%

Serve with:

Salmon with Appeal (p. 6)

Roast Garlic Chicken (p. 14)

Fried Rice (p. 32)

▼

White Chocolate Mousse

Ingredients:

**1 oz. White Chocolate
(or 57 White Chocolate Chips)**

**1/2 cup Whipped Cream
(prepared non-dairy)**

1 Lemon

Instructions:

Melt the chocolate over low heat or in the microwave for 3 minutes. Stir when done and allow to cool slightly. Mix in the whipped cream and 1 teaspoon of juice from the lemon until mixture is smooth. Pour into a tall martini glass. Cut a 1/2" square of the outside of the lemon peel (just the top layer of the lemon peel, called the zest, not the white below it) and sliver it into small pieces. Place on top of mousse mixture. Top with a single mint leaf.

Comments:

This dessert can be enjoyed warm off the stove or chilled, but the consistency will thicken as it cools. If you like the lighter consistency and want to cool the dessert, add an additional 2 tablespoons of whipped cream.

Nutritional Information:

	Chocolate	Cream
Fat 11 g	8	3
Calories	160	50
Fat Percent	45%	54%

Serve with:

Veal Piccata (p. 4)

Lamb Chops with Shallot (p. 7)

Fried Rice (p. 32)

▼

Strawberries and Cream

Ingredients:

1/2 cup Strawberries (9 of them)

2 tablespoons Cream

1 teaspoon Amaretto

Instructions:

Combine the cream and amaretto. Place strawberries in a nice wine glass and add cream and Amaretto mixture. Stir gently.

Comments:

This is similar to the Berries in double cream that starts off the breakfast at Brennen's in New Orleans. It may be a bit much for breakfast, but it's great for dessert.

Nutritional Information:

	Cream
Fat 12 g	12
Calories	108
Fat Percent	100%

Serve with:

Lemon Chicken (p. 2)

Pasta Quick (p. 3)

Steak Diane (p. 23)

Baked Apple

Ingredients:

1 small Apple (Stayman's are best)

1 tablespoon Butter

1 tablespoon Sugar

Instructions:

Preheat oven to 400°. Peel the top half of the Apple. Cut the stem out of the top by cutting around and into the apple for about 1/2". Place Apple, open side up, in a small oven proof bowl. Place butter and sugar in opening on top. Add enough water to bowl so that the bottom 1/2" of the apple is sitting in water. Put Apple in the oven. Bake 18 minutes. Remove to a serving plate.

Comments:

This is yet another apple recipe that goes well with the extra calories of a scoop of high quality vanilla ice cream.

Nutritional Information:

	Apple	Butter	Sugar
Fat 12.7 g	.4	12.3	0
Calories	81	111	46
Fat Percent	4%	100%	0%

Serve with:

Lamb Chops with Shallot (p. 7)

Lemon Chicken (p. 2)

Roast Garlic Chicken (p. 14)

Parfait Flambé

Ingredients:

1 Chocolate-coated Vanilla Ice Cream bar (such as Dove or Klondike)

2 tablespoons Grand Marnier liquor, room temperature

Instructions:

When ready to serve, place the ice cream in a dessert bowl. Add the Grand Marnier (it must be at room temperature) and ignite with a match. Using a large spoon, begin scooping the liquor onto the top of the dessert. Do this continually until the chocolate coating has dissolved and the flames have subsided. Run spoon under cool water, and serve dessert with a small spoon.

Comments:

This is based on a classic dessert (by the same name) found in all Swiss restaurants. The orange liquor and melted chocolate form an incredible sauce that is eaten with the vanilla ice cream. High-quality ice cream is the key. The bite-size chocolate-covered ice cream treats which have become popular recently work very well for this dessert; use about four small bite-size pieces.

Nutritional Information:

	Ice Cream
Fat	20 g	20
Calories	280
Fat Percent	64%

Serve with:

Lemon Chicken (p. 2)

Veal Piccata (p. 4)

Lamb Chops with Shallot (p. 7)

▼

Pears in Kahlúa Chocolate Sauce

Ingredients:

1 oz. semi-sweet Chocolate

1 tablespoon Coffee (brewed)

1 teaspoon Kahlúa liquor

1 cup Pear Slices (canned)

Instructions:

Over low heat in a sauce pan melt the chocolate (57 semi-sweet chocolate chips will do nicely). Remove from heat when shiny and stir quickly. Add the coffee and Kahlúa and stir until smooth. Place pears in small serving bowl, being sure to drain off the liquid syrup they are packed in. Top with sauce.

Comments:

To cut the fat content of this recipe, substitute no-fat chocolate syrup for the chocolate.

Nutritional Information:

	Chocolate
Fat 7.8 g	7.8
Calories	140
Fat Percent	50%

Serve with:

Lamb Chops with Shallot (p. 7)

Little Foot Pizza (p. 15)

Steak Diane (p. 23)

▼ Bad Baklava

Ingredients:

1 sheet Phyllo Dough

1/2 cup Brown Sugar

1/3 cup Walnuts, chopped

4 tablespoons Butter

1 tablespoon Honey

Instructions:

Melt butter. Blend sugar and walnuts together in a blender. Carefully lay out one sheet of Phyllo dough (18" x 14") on the counter. Brush half the dough with the melted butter. Fold the dough in half and brush again with butter. Spread one-fourth of the sugar mixture over half the dough. Fold over; brush and sugar again with one-fourth of the mixture. Do it one more time and place the 3" x 5" package in a cake pan. (Some sugar will remain.) Top with honey and bake 15 minutes. Cut into 2" squares and serve.

Comments:

This is <u>bad</u> baklava because traditional baklava takes infinite patience and contains infinite calories. Still, if you're watching your fat and calorie intake, don't even look at the nutritional data for this dessert!

Nutritional Information:

	Dough	Walnut	Butter
Fat 71.95 g	.25	22.7	49.0
Calories	45	240	339
Fat Percent	5%	85%	100%

Serve with:

Spaghetti with Mussels (p. 25)

Sea Bass á Teriyaki (p. 19)

Foiled Again Fillets (p. 5)

Other Info

Shopping Strategies

One of the most frustrating things about trying out new recipes is spending a fortune on the ingredients. How many times have you thought, "I could have eaten out for this much money." These shopping strategies will assure that you won't waste food or money. Although cookbooks often quote "only 40 cents a serving!", the check you write at the supermarket often says $40. If you have a good supermarket, and can use all of these strategies, you can make any meal in this book for $2 to $5, even in the most expensive grocery area of the country, Washington, DC.

Forget "Unit Pricing"

The fact that you are a smart consumer is probably costing you money. If you need milk for a recipe, a pint costs about $4 per gallon, while a gallon costs about $2.75, so generally shoppers opt for the larger sizes. However, if you throw out the milk after only using a pint (which is often the case), you are paying up to $20 a gallon for milk! Always buy the smallest unit of product you will use. It will be fresh and cost less in the long run, especially if you don't cook often. For example, if you are making the Fettuccine Alfredo, you may be better off buying a half pint of milk from the vending machine at work for 35 cents ($5.60 per gallon) than making a trip to the market for a gallon of milk that will go bad in a week.

Ask for what you need

Grocery stores assume most people are cooking for 4-6 people (as inaccurate as that is). Therefore, they package meats (chicken, lamb, etc.) for the convenience of those shoppers. That's why chicken breasts are packed in 4's and 6's. Grocers are more than happy to repackage meat in single packs if you ask. For example, if you need one chicken breast, ring the bell, hand the butcher the four pack and ask, "Can I have just one of these?" Nine out of ten will say, "Sure," with a smile. The tenth will say, "You bought that book! We're going to have to start putting out more meat prepackaged for one!" You can also ask for just a few slices of deli meat, cheese, or small amounts of ground beef or fish.

Salad Bar

This is a favorite among fans of "TOO EASY GOURMET." Many supermarkets now have salad bars. This is a great place to get pre-cut, pre-washed, ready to use ingredients. For example, if you need 1 cup of broccoli florets for the Sesame Broccoli recipe, get it from the salad bar. At about $2 per pound it will cost about 16¢, and be ready to use for the recipe. Otherwise, you'll have to buy a whole broccoli at 80¢ per pound and spend $1. Additionally, you have to wash it, trim it and throw out the 50% of the broccoli (the heavy stem) that is inedible. And you'll still have some leftover.

Onions, mushrooms, tofu, orange slices, vegetable oil and a variety of other ingredients are also usually available at good supermarket salad bars.

Bulk Foods

This is the author's favorite trick. Many large supermarkets now have a section that sells "bulk foods." These are top-quality foods that are sold by the pound in barrels rather than packaged. Since the packaging is a large part of the price you pay for many products, consumers gain by buying out of barrels by weight, without the packaging. You scoop the product into plastic bags and mark them. Your savings can be up to 200%. The products range from cookies to flour and from spices to dog bones. This is great for single cooks, especially in the area of spices. A bottle of spice (e.g. oregano) stays fresh only about 3 months in a cool dry place, (yes, check your cabinet!) and costs about $2.50 per bottle. In bulk, you can buy 1 tablespoon of fresh spice for about 4 cents! Grocers keep the products fresh and clean. Then they get to throw them out instead of you. Now you understand why buying four spices for one recipe makes your bill so high. You are already paying $10 in spices. With this strategy, you pay about 20¢ and everybody wins: you, the grocer, and the company that makes spices.

Break Packages

Most supermarkets permit you to break egg packages in half so you only buy six. A dozen eggs will stay fresh two weeks, so why buy 12 if you will only use 4 in two weeks? The same goes for butter. Grocers usually allow you to buy 1 stick rather than four. We already discussed meats in the section called "Ask for what you need" above.

Stock up, NOT!

Most cookbooks tell you to plan your meals a week in advance (yeah, right) and give you a list of things to stock. This is not practical for most people who work and have busy schedules. You are much better off keeping this book in a convenient place, such as in your car, briefcase, or purse. On the days when you want to cook, shop for what you need for that day (and one or two other days if you are sure you will cook). That way, ingredients will be fresh and you'll have no waste. Also, if it turns out you don't like a particular recipe, your investment has been minimal. Stock only things that are very nonperishable, such as flour, dry pasta and liquors, (great for making sauces). Generally, avoid freezing. It kills the flavors.

Be Clever

Think. If you have pasta, cheese and flour at home, all you need for Fettuccine Alfredo is milk. The vending machine at work will have it and you don't even have to stop at the market. Do you need 1 tablespoon of soy sauce? How many packages are stuffed in your top drawer from the take-out Chinese meals you've had this week? There are many nontradi-

tional places you can get ingredients for dinner. That left over white rice you never eat from your Chinese take-out can be used the next day for fried rice or California Rolls. At all costs, avoid running around to multiple markets to get ingredients. Many cookbooks recommend you first go to the fish market, then the grocer, then the butcher...who has time to do this?

Timing is everything

Finally, try to shop off-peak: If you live in the suburbs and commute home from downtown, everybody in your town will be at the supermarket at 5:30 P.M. Is there a reasonable grocer near downtown where you can stop first, while everybody else rushes for the home market? Can you shop at lunch, at break, or in the morning, when the

supermarket is so empty you could bowl in the aisles? I especially like the morning, because you can pick up some fruit for your most important meal, breakfast, at the same time.

Techniques

Browning–The purpose of browning is to assure that a tender piece of meat (sirloin, pork loin) stays juicy inside when cooked. This is done by frying the meat in a pan for about one minute on each side (or until well-browned) on high heat. Both sides will turn dark, sealing in the juices without cooking the meat on the inside. Further cooking at lower heat will do this, without drying it out. Allow for a little smoke, but stop when the meat is dark.

Deglazing–The best tasting part of pan-fried food is the bits of well cooked meat and burned butter that stick to the inside of the fry pan, mixed with run off fat and butter. Deglazing is a method of getting all that flavor into a sauce that can be served with the meat. To deglaze, remove the pan from the stove after cooking and add a small amount of lemon juice, wine, or broth. With a spatula, use the liquid to loosen up and scrape up all the flavor bits into a sauce. (Keep the pan off the stove or the liquid just evaporates away.) The amount of liquid determines the thickness of the sauce. To make it thinner, add more liquid. To thicken, heat to evaporate liquid intentionally, or add a small amount of flour.

Flambé–More than looking impressive, adding a liquor to food and igniting it actually caramelizes the sugars in the dish and adds a nice flavor, as well as leaving a hint of the liquor's flavor. It is relatively safe because alcohol burns at a low temperature. To flambé, be sure your liquor is at room temperature or slightly warmer. If it's too cold, it won't ignite; if it's too warm, it just evaporates off. Pour the liquid into the dish and touch a lit match to it. Tilt the pan and move the liquid around to keep the flame going as long as possible. (Note: AA doesn't recommend liquor in dishes for people with alcohol problems because it doesn't all burn off.)

Frothing Eggs–This makes egg whites into high, light meringue for dishes like soufflé and lemon meringue pies. The key is to start with room temperature egg whites in a large open bowl and get lots of air into the egg whites. Using a clean and very dry whisk or egg beater, start beating the egg whites at a slow speed. After about 30 seconds, change to high speed and do not stop until frothing is complete. Whites are done when they are stiff and opaque, with no visible bubbles and are just starting to be shiny. This takes about one minute when done with an electric mixer and about five minutes when done by hand. Handle the frothed egg whites as little as possible or they'll lose volume.

Grated Cheese–Rather than buying powdered cheese called grated cheese, always buy a piece of fresh cheese and grate it fresh with a small hand held grater. It is cheaper and far tastier, especially on pasta.

Juicing a Lemon–Roll the lemon (room temperature) on the counter under the palm of your hand with slight pressure. This will make it juicy. Cut and squeeze out the juice. Remove the seeds.

Making a Scaloppini–The purpose of this is to shape a piece of meat so that it is the same thickness all over and will cook evenly. Place the boneless meat between two pieces of wax paper to prevent sticking. Using a weight (meat mallet, rolling pin, Emmy award), pound the meat until it is evenly 1/4" thick.

No Brainer–Recipes that, after you have done them once or twice, you can do without ever having to refer to the recipe again.

Pasta, Cooking–Using a pot as large as possible, "boil water" on high. Add 1 teaspoon of oil. This will catch and collect loose flour from the pasta. Don't add salt; it doesn't do anything. Cook till tender, yet still firm to the bite. Do not over cook to the point where it is mushy. Drain cooked pasta through a colander. If you have used enough water, no rinsing is required.

Pasta, Storing and Recooking– Place cooked leftover pasta in an airtight storage container (such as a Ziplock™ bag or Tupperware™ container). Add about a teaspoon of vegetable oil and toss to coat pasta. Refrigerate. When ready to use, take out the amount needed and lower into a pot of boiling water using a colander or strainer for 30 seconds, or steam for about 2 minutes. Thin pasta may stick after refrigerating due to loose flour from cooking. Rinse in cold water to unstick before reheating.

Quick Cook Rice–Bring a pot of water to a boil. Add the rice and stir once or twice. Boil rice on high for 10 minutes then drain (just like pasta).

Sautéing–Cooking in an open fry pan over medium heat (for our recipes), with a small amount of butter or oil.

Separating eggs–Separating an egg means to divide it into its two parts: the yellow yolk (high fat), and the clear egg white (no fat), for separate uses. Cold eggs separate easily. Crack the egg in halves and keep the yolk in one half while you pour off the white into a bowl.

▼ Other Info

110

A clever trick if you have trouble doing this is to break the egg into a plastic funnel. The egg white will flow through and the yolk will remain in the funnel.

Steam(ing)–Steaming is a great way to cook with no fat. Put about 1" of water in a covered sauce pan over high heat. When it boils, add the food and cover again. Small metal steamers, Chinese baskets and baskets that will fit in the pan will help keep the food out of the water for steaming. Remember that steam is far hotter than boiling water so handle food and pans carefully.

Also, you can usually steam cook for no more than seven minutes or the pan will boil dry.

Water, Boiling–Fill pot with cold water and place on stove (open side up). Turn burner under pot on high. When water boils, lower heat to medium high.

Diet & Nutrition

Bottom line:

1 Your body needs food. Food is fuel.

2 If you want to be at an ideal weight and stay there for life, don't diet. Instead, you need to develop eating habits you can stick with and enjoy for life.

3 Fat in food makes you fat. Limit your fat and limit your weight. To maintain an ideal weight, the fat you take in by eating needs to be equal to the fat you lose by activity. How do you know what your fat intake should be? The following formula gives a general idea.

Your Daily Fat Intake

Your ideal weight   **Fat Grams**

_____ ÷ 2 = _____

Since TOO EASY GOURMET lists the total fat grams for each recipe, all you have to do is track how many fat grams you take in during the day and limit it to the above figure. This doesn't mean you have to banish all fats from your diet, but if you are planning to eat a pan of brownies for dinner, limit your fat for breakfast, lunch and snacks that day, so your total fat grams for the day do not exceed your budget. For more detail, (even if you hated those dreaded word problems in high school), read on.

The In/Out Factor

Weight gain and loss are both measured in calories. If you are a normally active person, you burn calories by being alive, and even by eating itself. Exercise will significantly increase calories (weight) lost. Eating high fat foods will significantly increase calories (weight) gained. Note: With age it naturally becomes harder to burn fat (lose calories) so activity must increase to maintain a balance (or to maintain the same weight).

How much fuel do you need?

Your body needs food to function properly. Many dieters think that since reducing calories will make them lose weight, severely reducing calories (dieting) will make them lose weight faster. However, your body is smart. It still has its "cave man" instincts. When you diet and your body isn't getting its minimum calories (the cave man can't find food), it kicks into the "energy saver mode," and starts storing all the fat it can. You can actually gain weight. When you go off the diet (the caveman finds a big woolly mammoth to eat) the body goes back to normal. This is known as yo-yo dieting, and studies have shown it is dangerous. How much fuel do you need? Again, this formula will give you a good figure to start with:

Your Daily Calories

Your ideal weight   **Daily Calories**

_____ x 15 = _____

What is Healthy?

All food is made up of three useful components: carbohydrates, proteins and fats. Most Americans eat too much fat, mostly in meat and dairy foods. According to studies by the American Heart Association, we get more than 40% of our calories from fats. We would be far healthier if we reduced our fat intake to less than 30% of total calories. Some studies suggest even lower figures. How do we determine what 30% of our calories is? Easy. On page 112, we have determined what our daily calories budget is, so (don't cringe, this is easy):

Daily Calories	Your Daily Calories from fat
_____ x .30 =	_____ cal.

and since each gram of fat equals 9 calories that means:

Daily Calories from fat	Daily Fat Intake
_____ ÷ 9 =	_____ gr.

And you'll notice that this number matches **Your Daily Fat Intake** from page 112. This shows how we got to that formula.

For More Accuracy

These formulas are rules of thumb and will get you started towards better health. You must consult a doctor or nutritionist for your specific situation. However, for more accuracy you can adjust as follows: the Metropolitan Life Height/Weight Chart is the standard used to suggest daily calories based on weight and activity. Instead of using 15 as the factor to determine your daily calorie intake, take the factor here:

	Sedentary	Active	Very Active
Female	12	15	16
Male	14	17	20

The "factor" is the number of calories you should eat per pound of your desired body weight.

Also, if you need a stricter limit on your fat intake, use a figure lower than 30% (.30) in the above formula. (Below 10% may not be healthy.) Then calculate your fat grams in the same manner (÷ calories from fat by 9).

Example 1: You want to be 120 lbs. You want to eat 30% or less from fat. Your fat gram limit is 60 grams per day. (120 x 15 x .30 ÷ 9 = 60)

Example 2: You want to be 135 pounds and want to restrict your fat intake to 20%. You are a sedentary female. Your fat gram limit is 36 grams per day. (135 x 12 x .20 ÷ 9 = 36)

Measurements

Your grandmother could cook without a book but when you asked her about measurements for her famous apple strudel she would look confused and say something like "oh, a little"...and "just enough". That didn't do you any good when you were standing over $40 worth of apples, sugar and flour getting ready to cook.

The recipes in all good cookbooks are painstakingly developed. Measurements of the ingredients are carefully determined. If you follow the directions and measurements exactly you should get great results, unless:

1) the recipe is not written clearly (see page 121),

2) ingredients were substituted (see "How to use this book"),

3) measurements were not made carefully.

Measurements: Volume and Weight

Food is measured in volume or weight and both can be measured in ounces. This can be confusing (i.e. 8 oz of Steak refers to 1/2 lb. and 8 oz. of milk refers to 1 cup of milk). Most supermarket items refer to liquids as fluid ounces (fl. oz.) to avoid confusion. You'll also notice that most foods are indicated by weight (oz.) except beverages, which are usually indicated by volume (fl. oz.).

Volume - The volume of food is measured in teaspoons, tablespoons, cups and ounces in the USA.

Standard Measure/Equivalent Volumes

1 Cup (1 C)	8 fl. oz.	16 T	48 t
1/2 Cup (1/2 C)	4 fl. oz.	8 T	24 t
1/4 Cup (1/4 C)	2 fl. oz.	4 T	12 t
1 Tablespoon (1T)	1/2 fl. oz.	3 t	
1 teaspoon (1 t)	1/6 fl. oz		

also: 1 Pint (Pt) = 2 Cups
2 Pints = 1 Quart
4 Quarts = 1 Gallon

How to measure - Slightly overfill the measuring cup or spoon, and then run a straight edge (like a wood ruler) across the top to scrape off the excess. This way you get a perfect measure. For liquid, read measuring cups at eye level. For chopped ingredients (like onions), chop first, then measure by filling cup snugly, but do not try to pack down the contents.

Weight - Food weights are measured in ounces (oz) and pounds (lbs) in the USA.

1 lb.	16 oz.
1/2 lb.	8 oz.
1/3 lb.	5.3 oz.
1/4 lb.	4 oz.

When the recipe suggests a specific weight of an item (potato, chocolate, onions) use the vegetable scale at the grocer to find one that meet your needs.

Suggested Menus

Notice too, that each main course recipe also lists suggested side dishes, appetizers and desserts that will go nicely with that recipe.

Low Fat Dinner (3.2 g)
Pasta Quick
Sesame Broccoli
Grand Marnier Oranges

Easiest (Least Work & Mess)
Asparagus Vinaigrette
Foiled Again Fish
Le Colonel

Most Clever Dinner
Hot Brie Dip
Salmon with Appeal
Peas in Zucchini Cups
Baked Alaska

Fewest Ingredients (6)
Orange Roughy
Asparagus Vinaigrette
Grand Marnier Oranges

Monday Night Football
Beer Boiled Shrimp
Little Foot Pizza
Quesedillas
Kahlúa Vanilla Nut

Kids' Menu
Macaroni & Cheese
Honey Beans
Apple Compote

Light Lunch
French Onion Soup
Good Salad
Peanut Butter Cookies

For Meat & Potato People
Steak Diane
Zoom Shrooms
Beer Boiled Shrimp
Oslo Ice Cream

Lowest Fat Main Dishes

Pasta Quick	2.6 g
Teriyaki Chicken	3.1 g
Spaghetti with Mussels	4.2 g
Sea Bass á Teriyaki	5.2 g
Roast Garlic Chicken	8.1 g
Little Foot Pizza	9.5 g
Tuna Steak	10.8 g
Lemon Chicken	11.31 g

Lowest Fat Desserts

Grand Marnier Oranges	0.2 g
Crêpes	0.3 g
Raspberry Sauce	0.3 g
Amaretto Strawberry	0.4 g
Le Colonel	1.5 g
Oslo Ice Cream	4.1 g
Chocolate Soufflé	7.8 g
Pears - Kahlúa	7.8 g

Lowest Fat Recipes

Honey Beans	0 g
Peas & Red Pepper	0 g
Grilled Eggplant Chips	0 g
String Bean Bundles	0.1 g
Sesame Lemon Spinach	0.2 g
Grand Marnier Oranges	0.2 g
Crêpes	0.25 g
Peas in Zucchini Cups	0.3 g

Most Fat
(Don't Ask / Don't Tell)

Bad Baklava	71.9 g
Tomato Mozzarella	56 g
Chocolate Fondue	56 g
Sweet Potato Side	50.5 g
Kahlúa Vanilla Nut	49 g
Lamb Chops with Shallot	48 g
Grilled Pizza	38.8 g
Chocolate Cream Pie	34.7 g

▼

Index

Recipe Index

How to comment on this book

If you find any recipe in this book unclear or incomplete please let us know so it can be corrected in future revisions. Our goal is to develop cookbooks that are easy to use. TOO EASY GOURMET has gotten better and better due to the feedback of its supporters. You can contact us via mail, fax and e-mail at the addresses on this page with your comments or suggested revisions.

Share your recipes and strategies for our future books

Too Easy Gourmet is quickly becoming a team effort. Everybody seems to have great ideas, strategies and recipes for quick and easy cooking. If you have recipes that you use or have developed that are quick and easy, and you want to share them in our next book, please send them and if we use your recipe we will give you credit in our next book. Fans of "Non-Fiction Cooking" are the ones who are making this concept great.

(TEG cannot acknowledge each submission and cannot return unused recipes. All recipes become the property of Too Easy Gourmet.)

Too Easy Gourmet Mailing List

To find out about Too Easy Gourmet news, workshops taking place in your area, advance notice of upcoming books, and discounts on future books, get on our mailing list by sending your contact information to one of the addresses below.

Ben Levitan's next book of non-fiction recipes will be out soon, adding more quick and delicious recipes to your personal repertoire.

Too Easy Gourmet Contact Information:

Mail:
TOO EASY GOURMET
PO Box 469, Annapolis, MD
21404

Fax:
(410) 266-0986

E-Mail:
ezgourmet@aol.com

Phone:
1-800-EASY-GOURMET
(1-800-327-9468)

Coming Soon!

Too Easy Gourmet II

More Non-Fiction Recipes

ISBN # 0-9640023-1-0

Other Info ▼

121

How to Order more copies of "Too Easy Gourmet – The world's first non-fiction cookbook" ISBN No. 0-9640023-0-2

Please mail me_____ copies at $6.95 each= _____

Sales Tax Please add 5% (35¢ per book) for books shipped to Maryland addresses _____

Shipping: For priority mail: Add $3 for up to 5 books and $1 for each additional book _____

For ground mail: Add $2 for the first book and $1 for each additional book _____

TOTAL: _____

Place your order today!

1-800- Easy-Gourmet

1-800-327-9468

Payment Method

❏ Check enclosed   ❏ Money Order enclosed   ❏ Credit Card: ❏ Master Card ❏ Visa

Credit Card Number ⊔⊔⊔⊔ ⊔⊔⊔⊔ ⊔⊔⊔⊔ ⊔⊔⊔⊔   Expiration date: _____

Name on card _____

Please ship my book to:

Name _____

Address_____**City**_____**State**_____ **Zip**_____

❏ **FAX ORDERS:** Fax this form to (410) 266-0986

❏ **MAIL ORDERS:** Mail to: **Too Easy Gourmet** PO Box 469, Annapolis, MD 21404

❏ **E-MAIL:** E-mail the above information to ezgourmet@aol.com

❏ **PHONE ORDERS:** Call 1-800-327-9468